Walking Tours
—of—
Old New Orleans

Walking Tours
—of—
Old New Orleans

by Stanley Clisby Arthur

Edited by Susan Cole Doré

PELICAN PUBLISHING COMPANY
GRETNA 2012

First published as *Old New Orleans* by Harmanson, Publisher 1936

First edition, 1936
Second printing, 1936
Third printing, 1936
Anniversary edition, 1937
Fifth printing, 1937
Second edition, August 1944
Seventh printing, November 1946
Eighth printing, November 1948
Ninth printing, November 1950
Tenth printing, August 1952
Eleventh printing, February 1954
Twelfth printing, September 1955
First Pelican edition, January 1990
Fourteenth printing, September 1995
Fifteenth printing, June 2003
Sixteenth printing, August 2008
Seventeenth printing, December 2011

Library of Congress Cataloging-in-Publication Data

Arthur, Stanley Clisby.
  Walking Tours of Old New Orleans / by Stanley Clisby Arthur ; edited
by Susan Cole Doré.—1st Pelican ed.
    p.   cm.
  Includes index.
  ISBN 978-0-88289-740-0
  1. Vieux Carré (New Orleans, La.)—Description—Guide-books.
2. Vieux Carré (New Orleans, La.)—History. 3. Historic buildings—
Louisiana—New Orleans—Guide-books. 4. New Orleans (La.)—
History. 5. New Orleans (La.)—Description—Guide-books.
I. Doré, Susan Cole. II. Title.
F379.N56V529 1989
976.3'35—dc20   89-31668
                                                                        CIP

Printed in the United States of America

Published by Pelican Publishing Company, Inc.
1000 Burmaster Street, Gretna, Louisiana 70053

Contents

Preface

IN 1936, STANLEY CLISBY ARTHUR set out to write an architectural guidebook describing the Vieux Carré, or French Quarter, of New Orleans. The Vieux Carré of Arthur's experience was a picturesque place of crumbling buildings, which, for the most part, had been abandoned by the well-to-do and left to shopkeepers, immigrants, and the poor. Many of the grand houses of the Creole elite were occupied by restaurants, antique shops of every description, and tenements. Some were simply vacant. Arthur described that Depression-era French Quarter in these words:

> Many doors are shut and clamped and grayed with cobwebs. Many windows are nailed fast. Half the balconies are begrimed and the iron railings rusteaten, and humid arches and alleys which characterize the older Franco-Spanish piles of stuccoed brick betray a fatalistic squalor.

For all its "fatalistic squalor," the Vieux Carré of 1936 was still permeated by a transcendental beauty. Block after block of graceful buildings remained after the exodus "uptown," and damp patios brimming with the scents of jasmine and sweet olive waited patiently to be discovered by artists and writers such as Lyle Saxon, Tennessee Williams, Sherwood Anderson, and William Faulkner. This verdant, aged Vieux Carré was the place Arthur wished to introduce and document in his guidebook.

Today the Vieux Carré remains a place of inestimable beauty, and the buildings which line its streets are testimony to the power of concerned preservationists. The same economic depression which gave Stanley Arthur a federal job as an archivist also spawned a preservation movement in the "Old Square," spearheaded by the Historic American Buildings Survey, directed in New Orleans by architect Richard Koch. New Orleanians, many of whom loved the French Quarter from afar in their homes in the Garden District, rallied to the plea Koch made for preservation action. Slowly but surely, money came back into the French Quarter, and the sagging nineteenth-century buildings took on new lives and purposes. The city of New Orleans established the Vieux Carré Commission, which has a legal mandate for the preservation of the *tout ensemble* of the French Quarter, and the coalition of public and private preservationists has transformed the Vieux Carré of Arthur's experience into a place of cherished antiquity and economic vitality.

Decades have elapsed since the last edition of *Old New Orleans* was published. The 1936 edition quickly became a collector's item, and the sixth edition, revised by Arthur in 1944, was reprinted six times, the last in 1955. This thirteenth edition is based upon the 1955 printing of the 1944 revised work. In his revision, Arthur added new material, and because of wartime printing restrictions, he condensed some of the entries that appeared in the original 1936 edition.

This edition of *Old New Orleans* is true to Arthur's original. Some changes have been made to make this book understandable and enjoyable for contemporary readers and "walkers" of the Vieux Carré. Some minor changes in address, reflecting the numbers one would see on buildings today, have been added. All were verified by "a pedestrian researcher" and by reference to the *Vieux Carré Survey*, a thorough catalog of French Quarter buildings housed at the Historic New Orleans Collection. Changes in punctuation which affect clarity have been made.

Some dramatic changes have taken place in the French Quarter since 1936 and 1944, and these have been noted. The 100 block of Royal Street presents a very different face from that described by Arthur; a Holiday Inn now occupies the sites of 116-126 Royal Street. Arthur's descriptions of the buildings that used to be there are present in this edition, and their demise is mentioned at the end of the entries. In Arthur's day two "gaps" existed in the Vieux Carré that contemporary visitors find difficult to imagine. The site of the Saint Louis Hotel, at the downtown river corner of Royal and St. Louis streets, was from 1915 until 1960 a parking lot surrounded by a board fence, and is now occupied by the Royal Orleans Hotel. The uptown "woods" or "lake side" corner of Bourbon and Toulouse streets was the site of the French Opera House, which burned in 1919, and when Arthur compiled his history of the Vieux Carré that corner was "a great vacant lot, surrounded by a high fence and filled with the wreckage of many other old-time edifices. . . ." A hotel now dominates that site, surrounded by strip-tease joints and ersatz "Cajun" cafes. References to the current uses of these buildings have been kept to a minimum and are mentioned only when it is important to the contemporary reader.

Readers will note Arthur's explanation of the directional terms "woods side" and "river side" in his foreword to this book. Most New Orleanians now call the "woods side" (the east) "lake side." The area beyond Rampart Street which Arthur described as "cane fields and forest lands" is today a well-developed business and residential area extending to Lake Pontchartrain.

This edition of *Old New Orleans* has benefited immeasurably from the generous and patient assistance of Pamela Arceneaux, reference librarian at the Historic New Orleans Collection.

SUSAN COLE DORÉ

Stanley Clisby Arthur

STANLEY CLISBY ARTHUR WAS a man of many talents. Perhaps his most remarkable talent was his ability to delve into neglected historical sources and give life to the facts within in writing that was uniquely his own. Arthur was an ornithologist, naturalist, and archivist, but in New Orleans he is best remembered as a chronicler of the city's families, architecture, and traditions.

Stanley Arthur was born in California in 1880, and he worked as a journalist in California, Texas, and New York before he came to Louisiana in 1915. He served as state ornithologist from 1915 until 1920, and it was during this period that he wrote *The Birds of Louisiana*, a catalog of the state's avian inhabitants, and a historical monograph, *The Story of the Battle of New Orleans*. In 1919, Arthur was chosen to be one of the naturalists accompanying the Seaman expedition into the interior of Labrador. Upon his return from Labrador he served as director of the Louisiana Conservation Department, Division of Wildlife, from 1924 until 1928.

Arthur had fallen passionately in love with his adopted state, and his fascination with her history resulted in the 1931 publication of *Old Families of Louisiana,* a genealogical narrative of the histories of Louisiana's founding families, which he coauthored with George Campbell Huchet de Kernion. As it did for so many writers, painters, and architects, the public works projects of the Great Depression gave Arthur the opportunity to discover his true métier. In 1934 he was appointed regional director of the Survey of Federal Archives, and from 1934 until 1940, Arthur became intimately involved with the history of New Orleans, cataloging and transcribing the city's rich notarial archives. His love of New Orleans and his access to the archives resulted in *Old New Orleans: A History of the Vieux Carré, Its Ancient and Historical Buildings*. It was first published in 1936, revised in 1944, and reprinted many times.

In 1937 Arthur published his most recognized work, *Audubon: An Intimate Life of the American Woodsman*. His biography of the famous artist and naturalist was lauded as a refreshing view of John James Audubon's life and works because it drew from Audubon's own letters and writing. The *Saturday Review of Literature* recognized the archivist in Arthur in a review published January 24, 1937:

> Whenever possible, Mr. Arthur has drawn, not only on the editorially "improved" printed version of Audubon's journals, but on the originals with all their quaintness of orthography and anarchy of grammar. These records he has supplemented with heretofore unpublished letters and he has filled in the backgrounds of his portrait through the testimony of those who intimately knew the naturalist.

It was fitting that Arthur, who had so closely studied the bird life of Louisiana, should choose to explore the life of Audubon, and it is not surprising that he should choose to be so faithful to the historical evidence of the naturalist's life.

Arthur's efforts to preserve Louisiana's documentary heritage led to his appointment in 1940 to the Board of Curators of the Louisiana State Museum. He became the museum's executive director in 1941 and served until his retirement in 1948.

Stanley Clisby Arthur was a prolific researcher and writer, and before his death at the age of eighty-three, he also published *The Fur Animals of Louisiana* (1931); *The Story of the West Florida Rebellion* (1935); *Famous New Orleans Drinks and How to Mix 'Em* (1937); *Louisiana Tours* (1950); and *Jean Laffite, Gentleman Rover* (1952).

Stanley Clisby Arthur died in New Orleans on December 4, 1963.

Foreword

BRIMMING WITH THE ROMANCE of 200 years, New Orleans merits the right to be called "America's Most Interesting City." This romance lingers on through the invasion of progress and the stamp of standardization. In the lower side of its broad bisecting Canal Street, old New Orleans is steeped in memories; on the upper side the New Orleans of today presents a picture of modern homes and gardens.

Interest for visitors centers in the *Vieux Carré,* which means literally, "Old Square," and is the part of the city originally founded. Here stands the *Cabildo,* where the colony of Louisiana was transferred from Spain to France, and by France transferred to the United States. Beside it the Saint Louis Cathedral silhouettes three tapering spires against the Creole sky.

In Jackson Square, now a pleasant loitering place of trees and flowers, a bronze General Jackson sits forever upon his bronze horse, and beyond and around this central point the old streets wander away into pathways of romantic history.

In no other city in this country do tradition and progress confront each other so definitely and as uniquely as in New Orleans. Second port in the United States, this old-world city yields no first position in the annals of romantic lore, or as a place where one may dine and wine extremely well.

Visitors asking directions are frequently mystified by the expressions "woods side" and "river side." These naive terms are local parlance for east and west. On the woods side, properly east, stand the cane fields and forest lands, and on the river side, or west, the Mississippi River flows past New Orleans in a graceful curve giving origin to the descriptive name of "Crescent City," by which New Orleans is familiarly known.

For the illumination of the uninitiated and misinformed, it must be stressed that the word *Creole* means French or Spanish or a mixture of these races, and far from being one of colored blood, the New Orleans Creole is a product of our exclusive and clannish strata of society. The Creoles founded New Orleans and it was their home a hundred years before the Americans came. Probably the misinterpretation of the word "Creole" grew from the Creole dialect spoken by the slaves of the

11

time and bears the same relation to purely spoken French as the Southern black dialect bears to English correctly spoken.

The purpose of this book is to present as accurate and as true a record of places and traditions in the Vieux Carré as has been possible to compile from painstaking research, and to design it for whoever may be as interested in the origin of facts as in the facts themselves.

The reader will doubtless find that many of the facts pertaining to the places of interest in the Vieux Carré differ from the usual information found in other books written about the old buildings of the original city. Unfortunately, as in other cities, many of the hoary traditions that have grown up about these buildings are demolished—traditions that fade when the pitiless light of fact is turned on their actual history and antiquity.

Old New Orleans has been compiled chiefly from ancient notarial acts; in every case the history of each old home has been searched through these conveyance records to establish original ownership and the year of actual building. Therefore, if blame for blasted tradition is to be attached to anyone it should be placed on the shoulders of the notaries of a century or more ago who set down in their seared and yellowed files actual transactions when both *pesos* and *piastres* were exchanged for land or building or both.

I will tell my story of the Vieux Carré only as I gleaned it from several hundred authentic sources. Most of them were dim words in French and Spanish on rotted paper traced by the crow quills of notaries in those distant times when strange flags—the golden lilies of Bourbon France, the square red and white banner of Castile and Leon, the red and yellow Bars of Aragon, and the fifteen stars and fifteen stripes of the young United States—floated over old New Orleans from the tall staff in the center of *La Place d'Armes*.

Walking Tours
—of—
Old New Orleans

The Founding of
New Orleans

LOUISIANA, NAMED FOR LOUIS le Grand, the fourteenth of his name to rule France, was settled in 1699 by Pierre Le Moyne, Sieur d'Iberville, a Canadian who was accompanied on this momentous mission by his younger brother, Jean Baptiste Le Moyne, Sieur de Bienville. Both left their names written large on pages of the state's history.

The city of New Orleans, however, did not have its beginnings until 1717, a year earlier than commonly set down in history books. It was in that year that Bienville, whose elder brother had in the meantime died, was directed to remove the seat of government of the Louisiana colony from the new Biloxi Fort on the Gulf Coast to a location on the *Fleuve Saint-Louis*, as the French had renamed the Indians' *misi sipi*, or "great water." The site he had selected was at an old Indian portage leading from the river to the big lake in the rear.

This new seat of government had been christened, in France, *Nouvelle-Orléans* four years before the dense growth of cypress trees and heavy subtropical underbrush had been cleared to lay out its streets. The name was bestowed in honor of His Highness, the then regent of France, Louis Philippe, duc d'Orléans, one of the greatest roués who ever stalked through the pages of history.

The use of the word *nouvelle*, feminine in spelling, prompted the Jesuit missionary Father Charlevoix, who reached the new capital at its beginnings in 1721, to comment:

> Here I am in this famous city which they call *Nouvelle-Orléans*. Those who have coined the name must have thought that Orleans was of the feminine gender. But what does it matter? The custom is established and custom is above the rules of grammar.

The explorer-priest had good reason for raising the point, as the general rule in French gives masculine preference to names of towns when derived from foreign names of masculine or neutral gender.

Whether feminine or masculine in baptism, the city of New Orleans was founded in 1717. Eighty illicit saltmakers, convicted and banished to the New

View of New Orleans in 1719

World for evading the French tax on salt, arrived in Louisiana and, with their numbers reinforced by carpenters and other workmen, were dispatched to the old portage location on the banks of the big river destined to become the present New Orleans. Bienville summoned Jacques Barbazon de Pailloux from the fort he had already established at Natchez to govern the nascent town; therefore M. Pailloux may well be acclaimed the city's first citizen.

Unsympathetic with Bienville's selection of a site for the new seat of government for the colony, Le Blond de La Tour, sent to Louisiana as chief king's engineer, suggested another location, although he had never visited the banks of the Mississippi. The young governor, not to be balked in his intentions by an unfriendly recalcitrant, proceeded with his original plans. He ordered Adrien de Pauger, an assistant king's engineer who had arrived with his chief de La Tour at Biloxi in 1720, to go to the Mississippi River site and lay out a new city. This he did on March 5, 1721. Thus it was de Pauger, and not his immediate superior de La Tour, who usually is credited with first laying off the squares of the original town—the Vieux Carré of today.

From 1717 to 1721, the period before engineer de Pauger laid out the streets and islets in the embrace of the crescent bend of the mighty Mississippi, the city's first lowly habitations were clustered along Bayou St. John, near our present City Park.

New Orleans today is known by a number of sobriquets—America's Most Interesting City, Creole City, the City Care Forgot, Carnival City, Queen City of the South, and Crescent City, the last being the most fitting as well as the oldest. It gained this designation from the fact that the river here makes a crescent bend. Such a name was used by Bienville, the city's founder, on May 10, 1717, when he proposed to newly arrived Governor de l'Espinay that he knew the perfect natural site for the new capital he was ordered to establish. Bienville told the governor who was displacing him: *"Sur les bordes du fleuve [est] un endroit très propice pour établir un poste sur l'un des plus beaux croissants du fleuve."* [On the banks of the river is a place very favorable for the establishment of a post on one of the finest crescents in the river.]

When engineer de Pauger laid out the original streets and the limits of the city that was to be, the site took on the appearance of a huge square—so many blocks or *islets* long and so many blocks wide. Thus the original section of the city became known to the French-speaking population, in later years, as the *Vieux Carré* (Old Square), a name we reverently use today.

Therefore, welcome to old New Orleans and its colorful Vieux Carré.

The Houses of the Past

THE HOUSES BUILT BY the original French settlers and their children were low frame structures, bricked between posts and roofed with cypress shingles. The French designated this style of architecture *briqueté entre poteaux,* meaning literally, "bricked between posts." About 1770, during the time of the domination of Spain, the new buildings of the Vieux Carré took on increased ostentation. Many were constructed wholly of bricks, and when an occasional one was built two stories high it was more magnificently classified *une maison en brique et à étage* (a house of brick with one story). Tile was substituted for wooden shingles; some roofs were covered with the familiar half-round red tiles, others with flat green tiles. Age-worn examples of these flat tiles from Nantes and Havre still cover a few of the old homes and are well worth observing, especially after a rain when the sun shines on their wet surfaces and brings out the verdant color baked into them. Flat tiles were used on the roofs of house that were terraced and flower-planted after the manner of residences in Mexico City and Havana, and at sundown families repaired to these high places to enjoy what breeze might be meandering across the old town from the direction of the river.

No residence of the Old Square however grand or humble was without its courtyard or patio. Houses were built flush with the *banquette,* as the sidewalk was called. To gain entrance to the court one passed through the *porte cochère,* a wide gate usually constructed of thick planks, then through the high-domed passageway that tunneled the ground-floor structure. This corridor was sufficiently wide to admit a brace of horses drawing the family carriage called a *calèche découverte.* The opening to the patio was high enough to prevent the black coachman with his towering beaver hat from being knocked from his perch on the carriage seat.

To the French the flagged or bricked "backyard" was a *cour,* but with the coming of the Spanish the term *patio* was used and remained in favor. There was usually a fountain in the center of the patio and a well-planned garden or *parterre,* or at least a collection of potted plants to enliven the walled-in court with green leaves and bright flowers. Huge wide-mouthed and pot-bellied earthen jars that had carried overseas the oil from the olive groves of Spain found their way into the garden and were used to catch the rain water from the roof gutters and downspouts. Today the old jars or *ollas* are considered distinctly decorative features of any Old Square courtyard. Occupying one or two sides of the court were the kitchen and slave quarters, buildings always detached from the main dwelling, and in the rear were the carriage house and stalls for the horses.

The broad stairs which led to the living apartments of the main house were built in the patio under the shelter of a "gallery" or upstairs porch, but more usually they led upstairs from the corridor. Houses of true Spanish construction can be recognized at a glance by the window openings which are wide, arched at the top, and frequently without a prominent keystone. Over many, and especially above entrances indoors and out, are to be seen the celebrated fan transoms, distinctive features in these architectural relics of the old New Orleans Vieux Carré. Sills of the windows that opened on the courtyards were made generously wide to hold flower pots, for the Creoles were then as now fond of growing things, and few homes were without little pots of fragrant rosemary. Aside from its medicinal properties, rosemary was the "flower of remembrance" and was believed to keep an absent lover's thoughts continually on the fair one left behind. Consequently, these plants were diligently tended.

Two disastrous fires visited New Orleans during the Spanish regime, the first in 1788, the second in 1794. One of the orders issued by Governor the Baron de Carondelet after the second conflagration ordained that all homes in the center of the city, built more that one story high, be reconstructed of brick, and Spanish police regulations also decreed the kind of timber to be used—cypress which must be felled at certain periods of the year, and incredible but true, only during certain *phases of the moon!* It was believed that the wood thus secured would be well seasoned and free from decay. Today, notwithstanding the inroads of time and the ravages of age and a damp, subtropical climate, many of the buildings in the heart of the Vieux Carré remain remarkably preserved specimens of the splendid architecture of the Spanish Creoles.

The bricks used in the construction of these buildings were made from a peculiar sandy clay found along the banks of the Mississippi and even within the embrace of the famed crescent bend. When removed from the kilns, the bricks had a peculiar texture—they could be rubbed together and reduced, without much effort, to a mass of yellowish-red powder. Yet they served their purpose admirably when employed in erecting high buildings. To make one brick adhere to another, a native cement or mortar was used. It is claimed that the secret of this cement has been lost, like that of the old Roman cement used in building the *Via Appia*, but chemists of today know why this cement of the builders of 1795 compares in hardness and durability with materials now in use. This mortar of old New Orleans was made from lime secured by burning the clam shells still abundant in nearby Lake Pontchartrain and other lake bottoms. When unsaturated with moisture, this mortar becomes a binder even of harder substance than the bricks it holds so firmly together. However, to keep the soft bricks from eroding and the mortar from becoming wet, it was found neccessary to plaster the exterior of the structure. That is why the old buildings of the French Quarter are always covered with plaster, and why, when the plaster has fallen away in patches on some ancient structure, the exposed bricks are worn and rounded from the rain and the mortar has crumbled from between them. In 1805, bricks from Holland were widely used.

Balconies, the *miradors* of the Spanish and *galeries* of the French, were placed on all houses more than one story high and were a necessity in a hot climate. In time they became objects of beauty and the pride of the householder. Homeowner strove with homeowner to outdo one another in the design of this outward badge of affluence. Many had their initials forged into the design and a few of these artistic and priceless monograms, wrought-iron mementos of a glorious past, remain to tell of a golden era in old New Orleans.

There are two kinds of iron decorations on the balconies of the Vieux Carré—the wrought iron of the period from 1795 to 1830, and the cast-iron "lacework" that came into favor about 1830, although the first cast-iron balcony grillage was imported from England in 1810, and customs manifests of 1825 prove that English cast-iron came into this port in considerable quantities that year.

Although it has been freely stated that the splendid examples of wrought iron on the balconies of many of the more ancient edifices of the Old Square were hammered out here on the anvils of slave *forgerons* or by the brothers Laffite, it now appears they were the work of neither slave nor pirate, nor were they even made here. These wrought-iron decorations, imported from southern Spain and freighted over the ocean from Cadiz, were probably the output of some *herreria* in the vicinity of Seville. For the iron used in making these balcony railings was of the puddled slag-bearing metal containing practically no carbon—that is why it does not rust—and which has a grain somewhat like that contained in wood. In the early days there were no iron ore deposits in the vicinity of Louisiana and iron for any purpose had to be imported from the Old World. So, designs were drawn and measurements for balcony grilles sent to Spain, and the finished product came back

Wrought-iron bracket supporting the balcony at 413 Royal St.

from Cadiz on sailing ships and was put in place on the balconies of the Old Square. The best of the old wrought-iron balcony decorations are therefore, in more than one way, pure Castilian.

Cast iron, on the other hand, has a high carbon content and is an easier prey to rust. That is why it is kept painted on many of the houses it decorates.

Mardi Gras

TO AMERICANS MARDI GRAS means New Orleans, as in Europe the Carnival season evokes thoughts of Rome, Venice, and Nice.

The dictionary definition of Carnival—"the season or festival of merrymaking before Lent; any merrymaking, feasting, etc., when indecorous"—is a far cry from the prolonged period of pageantry, splendor, and social activity that is Carnival in New Orleans. The season begins early in January with the ball of the Twelfth Night Revelers, and from then to Ash Wednesday nearly two months later New Orleans surrenders itself to a hysteria of gaiety. Brilliant ball follows brilliant ball, given by various secret organizations, most of which have no other object of existence.

Literally translated, Mardi Gras means "Fat Tuesday" and is the French phrase for Shrove Tuesday. It comes just before the penitential Ash Wednesday, which begins the Lenten season. During the final week of the Carnival celebration the resident population, reinforced by thousands of visitors, look upon a city at play and giving expression to Latin instincts and traditions in a plethora of festivities and elaborate symbolical parades. On Mardi Gras day maskers throng the streets from sunup to sundown, merrymaking prevails, rich and poor alike mingle in the same amusements, and there is a champagne in the air that once experienced can never be forgotten.

The word "Carnival" takes its original meaning from the annual spring celebration that had its beginning 5,000 years ago when painted priests pursued naked shepherds over Arcadian hills and dales, lashing the fleeing guardians of the flocks with whips made from the skins of goats. This sadistic celebration was in the nature of a religious rite conceived for the purification of the soil, for better pasturage, and the remission of sins. In time the custom was taken to Italy and carried to depths so lewd that in the fifth century the Church, which had vainly tried to crush the festival, countered with a celebration of its own. It deftly turned a pagan custom into one with Christian significance and the original intent of remission of sin with a deeper sense of mitigation.

To this spring festival the Church gave the name *carnelevamen*, meaning "consolation of the flesh," and it was not long before the word was shortened to *carneval*.

21

Mardi Gras in 1871, Canal and St. Charles (drawn by J. Harley)

The fact that "*carnis*" means "flesh" and "*vale*" means "farewell" gave rise to the frequently repeated misstatement that carnival meant "farewell to flesh." The original and correct meaning is "consolation of the flesh."

Even before New Orleans was founded, the Mardi Gras was observed in Louisiana. When Iberville and Bienville made their first exploration of the Mississippi River they put up for the night on a small bayou, and because of the date in February, christened the stream "Mardi Gras Bayou." When the city was founded and colonists grew in number, every spring before the beginning of Lent the Carnival was fittingly observed by balls but not by any out-of-doors masking and merrymaking.

The year 1838 recorded the first masked parade of a band of young Creole gentlemen. It has been erroneously believed and publicized for decades that the original celebration of street maskers took place in 1827. This mistake of eleven years came about through a typographical error in an old New Orleans newspaper, and has been kept alive ever since by all who copied the account or copied the copies.

Another myth that persists has long claimed that young bloods who had just returned from Paris introduced the European custom of celebrating the final day of Carnival by masking and parading through the streets in fantastic dress. The myth goes on to claim they had planned this first Mardi Gras celebration in the dining rooms above the old Gem saloon in Royal Street. As a matter of fact, this "Gem" meeting was concerned in the organization of the Mistick Krewe of Comus and did *not* take place in 1827 but thirty years later—on January 10, 1857.

What was evidently the first planned Mardi Gras street procession was held on Tuesday, February 27, 1838, for a news item in the *Commercial Bulletin* the next day said in part:

> END OF CARNIVAL—The European custom of celebrating the last day of Carnival by a procession of masqued figures through the public streets was introduced here yesterday, very much to the amusement of our citizens. . . .

In spite of this "introduction," we find that a year before, on Ash Wednesday, February 7, 1837, the then just started newspaper, *The Picayune,* carried an account of what was probably the city's first open-air Carnival to be celebrated by noisy, masked, and costumed throngs:

> COWBELLION—A lot of masqueraders were parading through our streets yesterday, and excited considerable speculation as to who they were, what were their motives, and what upon earth could induce them to turn out in such grotesque and outlandish habiliments. Some said they were Seminoles; some said it was the Zoological Institute come to town; some said it was Brown's Circus—while others said nothing, and very likely knew nothing at all about it. Boys, negroes, fruit women, and what not, followed the procession—shouting and bawling and apparently highly delighted with the fun, or what is more probable, anxious to fill their pockets with sugar plums, kisses, oranges, etc., which were lavishly bestowed upon them by these good-hearted jokers, whoever they were. For ourselves, we hardly saw them; but from the noise and tumult they made we concluded that it was a cowbellion society turned loose in the street to practice their harsh discordant music.

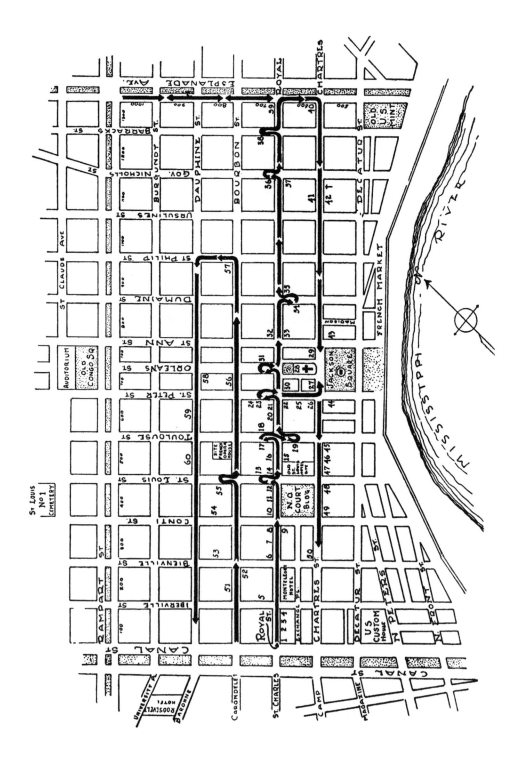

Two Walking Tours through Old New Orleans

LEGEND

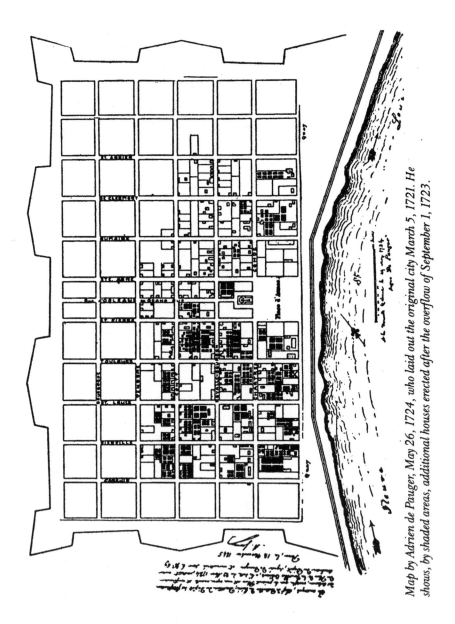

Map by Adrien de Pauger, May 26, 1724, who laid out the original city March 5, 1721. He shows, by shaded areas, additional houses erected after the overflow of September 1, 1723.

Street Names

THE EXCEEDINGLY NARROW STREETS—thirty-eight feet wide to be exact—of old New Orleans were laid out by Adrien de Pauger to meet the exigencies of a torrid climate, and by close juxtaposition benefit from the shade and protection afforded by adjacent buildings and overhanging balconies. Most of these streets, you will find, were named for members of the reigning family of France, their patron saints, the city's founder, and the faithful nuns who became the first teachers and nurses in Louisiana. In later years changes in naming were made to honor an American naval hero, a governor, and the founder of the Louisiana province.

ORLEANS STREET—*Rue d'Orléans* or *Grand rue*, as it was originally named by engineer de Pauger, was intended to become the city's main thoroughfare. He therefore laid it out with the then imposing breadth of forty-five feet, seven feet wider than the other streets. From the beginning, and for 109 years, *rue d'Orléans* started at the immediate rear of the parish church, and crossing *rue Royale*, cut directly through the exact center of the Vieux Carré.

DECATUR STREET—The first street facing the Mississippi River was originally the *rue du Quai* but later became known as *rue de la Levée*. In 1870 this important commercial street was renamed in honor of Stephen Decatur, the American naval hero whose daring exploit in the harbor of Tripoli had brought him fame.

CHARTRES STREET—The second street, counting from the riverfront, from the time of the establishment of the city bore dual names. From the church down to the lower boundary line it was *rue de Condé*, for the brawling French prince who espoused the niece of Cardinal Richelieu. From the church to the upper boundary line the street was *rue de Chartres*, named for the oldest of the Orleans princes. After the infiltration of the Americans it was called by many "Church Street" because the church faced it. In 1856 the city authorities decreed that for its full length, from Canal Street to the Esplanade, it should bear a single name—Chartres.

ROYAL STREET—The third street from the river was originally called *Royalle-Bourbon*, in honor of both the royal family and the dynasty. It did not carry this hyphenated name long for Bienville ordered it changed to *rue Royale* and so it has remained.

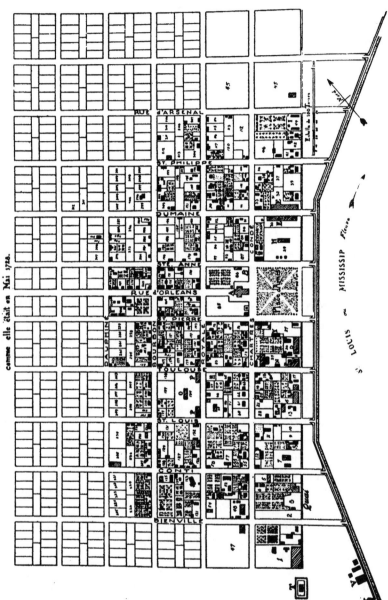

PLAN DE LA NOUVELLE ORLEANS
comme elle était en Mai 1728.

Old New Orleans as it looked May 15, 1728, from the original map by Ignace François Broutin

BOURBON STREET—First called Conti, in honor of the Princess Conti, this naming was changed to Bourbon when the hyphenated *rue Royalle-Bourbon* was not allowed to stand. The name of the princess was transferred to the street we today call Conti.

DAUPHINE STREET—The fifth street from the river was originally *rue de Vendôme*, named for the French general of the same name, but it was later changed to *rue Dauphine*, supposedly for the Dauphiness. Another version holds to the theory that the street was named for the French province of Dauphiné and, therefore, should be pronounced "Dau-phi-NAY" and not "Dau-FEEN," as presently heard.

BURGUNDY STREET—From the very beginning this street was *rue de Bourgogne*, merely the Gallic spelling of the name, and it has never been called anything else.

RAMPART STREET—*Rue des Remparts* acquired its name from the ramparts which guarded the city from the rear.

CANAL STREET—This name was not included in de Pauger's original nomenclature. At one time a wide canal drained off excessive rain water in this area so this explains the name fastened to the chief business thoroughfare. Its earliest name was *Canal des Pêcheurs*. In 1830 its banks were often designated *la promenade publique* along which strolled the socially elect while fishermen plied their trade in the middle of the "street."

IBERVILLE STREET—While named for the "father of Louisiana" it did not bear his name until 1901. Prior to that year it was called *Nueva Duaña* by the Spanish, then rue *de la Douane* by the French, and when the Americans came it became "New Custom House Street" because the new Spanish Custom House faced it.

BIENVILLE STREET—This was named for the "father of New Orleans." Originally it was called *rue d'Anguin* (de Pauger's misspelling for the duc d'Enghien, eldest son of the Prince of Condé). Bienville's name had then been given to the street we now call Conti. When Conti was changed to Bourbon, and the name of the Princess Conti transferred to the street now bearing her name, Bienville's name was given to the street now bearing it.

CONTI STREET—Originally called *rue de Bienville*, its change to Conti has already been explained.

ST. LOUIS STREET—*Rue Saint-Louis* was named for Louis IX, patron saint of France, of New Orleans, of the church of the diocese, and in addition, his name was fastened on the river that flowed past the city—*Fleuve Saint-Louis* instead of the Indians' name of Mississippi.

ST. PETER, ST. ANN, and ST. PHILIP STREETS—As the patron saints of the House of Orleans were Saint-Pierre, Sainte-Anne, and Saint-Philippe, for whom the royal offsprings were named, it is not strange that the pious de Pauger had these saints in mind when he gave these three streets the names they bear today. On an original early map, however, *rue de Clermont* (after Robert, comte de Clermont, sixth son of Saint-Louis and head of the Bourbon line) appears to have been the name first attached to the street afterwards designated *Saint-Philippe*.

TOULOUSE and DUMAINE STREETS—These streets were named for the royal bastards, duc de Toulouse and duc du Maine, sons of Louis XIV and Mme de Montespan. In the closing days of the Spanish domination *rue du Maine* was renamed *calle de los Almacenes* or, as we would say it, "Magazine Street." The original French name was restored in 1803, but we today call it *Dumaine* instead of translating it "Main Street."

URSULINES STREET—On Adrien de Pauger's original plans it will be noted that this was *rue Saint-Adrien,* in honor of his own patron saint, but not for long. It was changed to *rue de l'Arsenal,* then became *rue Sainte-Ursule,* and finally *rue des Ursulines,* named for the order of nuns whose chapel faced this street.

GOVERNOR NICHOLLS STREET—This was the second street to be called *rue de l'Arsenal* but its name was changed to *rue de l'Hôpital* because the King's Hospital faced it. After being known as Hospital Street for 180 years it was renamed in 1911 to honor Francis Tillou Nicholls, twice chief executive of Louisiana.

BARRACKS STREET—When laid out and named by the Spanish in 1792 it was called *calle Duaña,* meaning "Custom House Street," but in 1795 it was renamed *calle Quartel,* which the French-speaking folk translated to *rue de Quartier* because the barracks or quarters for the troops faced it. When the Americans came they called it "Garrison Street" but soon the name "Barrack" again came into popular use and in late years a final "s" has been added.

ESPLANADE AVENUE—This avenue, properly "the Esplanade," was so called because the *esplanade* or parade lay immediately beyond the lower boundary.

The Vieux Carré

THERE IS NO MORE DELIGHTFUL guide to the Vieux Carré than George W. Cable, author of many charming tales of old New Orleans. His characters of fiction have become almost as real as the places in which he made them live and love.

Let us start from Canal Street and saunter with Cable into the quiet, narrow way which devotees of Creole antiquity, in fondness for a romantic past, are still prone to call *rue Royale*. We will pass a few restaurants, a few auction rooms, a few shops, furniture warehouses, and many antique shops, and presently we will find it difficult to credit we have left behind us the activity and clatter of a city of merchants as we enter "a region of architectural decrepitude where an ancient and foreign-seeming domestic life in second stories overhangs the ruins of a formal commercial prosperity, and upon everything has settled a long sabbath of decay."

Many doors are shut and clamped and grayed with cobwebs. Many windows are nailed fast. Half the balconies are begrimed and the iron railings rust-eaten, and humid arches and alleys which characterize the older Franco-Spanish piles of stuccoed brick betray a fatalistic squalor. Yet, as Cable found it in 1870, beauty and the picturesque still linger here, which the blare of invading radios and smart reconditioning of crumbling facades seem only to emphasize by contrast. Occasionally you get a glimpse as he did of comfort, sometimes of opulence, through the unlatched wicket of some iron-barred doorway, of brick-reddened pathways, of dark palm or pale banana foliage, marble or granite masonry and blooming courtyards. Or through a chink between some pair of heavy batten window-shutters opened with a reptile wariness, your eye catches a glimpse of lace and brocade upholstery, silver and bronze, and similar rich antiquity.

Yes, the ancient street is at heart the same as Cable found it when he strolled along its narrow sidewalks—we call them *banquettes* in New Orleans, a Creole word of our own in its application. The true French word for sidewalk, *trottoir,* is never heard, for our inhabitants prefer to cling to the ancient designation applied by the first citizens of the little city. *Banquettes* were a series of raised planks that had to serve as footways because such "little bridges" were an absolute necessity to keep shoes out of the very mushy, water-soaked streets in the old days.

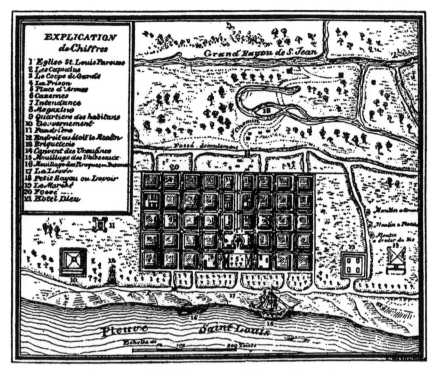

An early map of the Vieux Carré from the memoirs of Dumont de Montigny

Even against the inroads of commercialism there persists in *rue Royale* and the other streets of the Vieux Carré that Old World charm from which Cable wove his stories of Madame Delphine, 'Tite Poulette, Jean-ah Poquelin, Doctor Sevier, Posson Jone', and other pictures of the past. Here he looked with a calculating writer's eye on the building in which he housed Madame Délicieuse and 'Sieur George, and that low-roofed and balcony-shaded mansion in Dumaine Street which in his romantic imagination was "Madame John's Legacy."

A Walk Down Royal Street

ROYAL STREET IS SOMETIMES called the "Fifth Avenue" of old New Orleans for in this narrow thoroughfare are clustered many of the buildings occupied by the elite of the nineteenth century. The buildings, many of them, are still there even though traditions of a colorful past are the sole inhabitants of these once magnificently appointed mansions of a Creole aristocracy. Others are not only crowded with traditions of a colorful past but are jammed with antiques . . . outdated furniture that has lured many confirmed seekers of the elusive "real" antique.

If we are to explore the Vieux Carré on foot, and there is no other way really to see "Frenchtown," we start our sight-seeing promenade at Canal Street where Royal joins this busy thoroughfare, and, with Canal Street at our back, we will walk *downtown.*

As we saunter along its brief but fascinating length, we shall bear in mind that the houses are numbered *odd* on our left while even numbers will be across the street on our right, for we will keep, for convenience's sake, on the left *banquette* or sidewalk.

We are now in the famed Vieux Carré (pronounced *vieu* meaning "old," and *ca-ray,* which is French for "square"), the original city first laid out by engineer de Pauger in March of 1721.

The blocks are now numbered in units of 100—the first square, Canal to Iberville Street, is 100; from Iberville to Bienville, 200; from Bienville to Conti Street, 300; and so on. Brennan's Restaurant at 417 Royal Street will be found in the fourth block from Canal Street between Conti and St. Louis.

The same system of numbering pertains to the cross streets—the low numbers starting at the river and running "to the woods," thus the 700 block of all cross streets will be found between Royal and Bourbon streets, with all *odd* numbers on the *downtown* side, that is on the side towards Esplanade.

So we are ready to explore the length of one of the most interesting streets in America, old *rue Royale,* and see its old houses with overhanging balconies and wrought-iron railings, its courtyards and gardens, and its once-upon-a-time fashionable homes of the French and Spanish Creoles of *Nouvelle-Orléans.* We will see

33

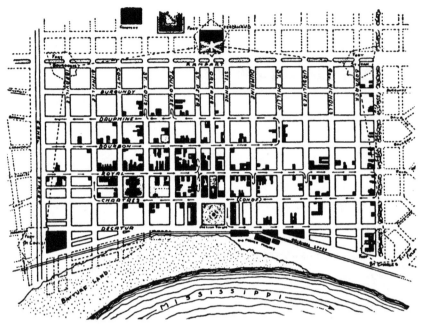

Map of the Vieux Carré of today and yesterday showing the location of the principal buildings of interest described in this work. The arrows indicate the walks to be taken to view the Old Square's historic edifices.

the antique shops, the tearooms, the old bookstores, the gift shops, the artists' studios, and the restaurants—all catering to and enticing the tourist, be he mere sightseer, lover of the historic and picturesque, or student of history. Every block of Royal Street will be teeming with interest.

THE GRANITE BUILDING   100 ROYAL ST.

Beginning our sight-seeing journey at the junction of Royal and Canal streets we can glance for a moment at the granite-faced building, three stories high, on the right-hand corner, known since its erection in 1833 as the Granite Building. The builder was Jean Baptiste Etienne Germain Musson, who purchased the site from the Widow Rillieux in 1811, when what is now Canal Street was known to the inhabitants as *la promenade publique*. It was not until 1833, however, that Germain Musson constructed this then pretentious structure—the first of its kind in the city to be built of Quincy granite from Yankee-land. Previously such building material came from across the sea as ballast in sailing ships that on their homebound voyage to England had their holds crammed with bales of cotton consigned to the looms of Liverpool and Manchester mills.

OLD COSMOPOLITAN HOTEL SITE   121 ROYAL ST.

The building which once housed the St. Regis restaurant and the Cosmopolitan

Hotel, a favorite rendevous in the gay nineties for gourmets and smart society folk, no longer exists, and the site is occupied by a modern hotel. The hotel was noted for its bar as well as its cuisine. Over meals washed down by suitable liquids, many a Central American revolution was hatched by Spanish-speaking guests.

In the stained-glass front of the St. Regis restaurant were three memorial windows honoring a trio of men who helped make the name of Louisiana known to the world. Two were native sons, Paul Morphy and Louis Moreau Gottschalk. For Morphy, peer of chess players, one window showed chessmen on a checkerboard. A second window, depicting "The Last Hope" on a sheet of music, was a tribute to Gottschalk, famed pianist and composer. The third window, picturing a singing mockingbird near a magnolia bloom, honored John James Audubon who, though not born in Louisiana, made in this state most of the bird drawings that brought him imperishable fame.

THE OLD SAZERAC   116 ROYAL ST.

On the right-hand side of Royal Street can still be seen the word "Sazerac" lettered in white tile on the sidewalk. This was the entrance that once led to a well-patronized bar on the Exchange Alley side of the building, now a part of a hotel. It was here in the good old days that a potent concoction famed far and wide as the Sazerac Cocktail was dispensed—it was here that it was so named. Old-timers will tell you the three distinctive drinks of New Orleans in the ken of living men were the dripped absinthe of the Old Absinthe House, the Ramos gin fizz, and the Sazerac Cocktail.

That pleasant institution known as the American cocktail was not only born in old New Orleans but was christened a "cocktail" in the Vieux Carré. The most famous of all cocktail drinks was the Sazerac and the fact that it originated here gave rise to the legend that it was named for a Creole family, a legend that has occasioned many a fruitless genealogical search as there was no such Louisiana family.

The original cocktail was a mixture of sugar, cognac, and aromatic bitters manufactured by a New Orleans druggist, A. A. Peychaud, and was known to those who first sampled the apothecary's mixture as a "brandy cocktail." One of the favorite brands of cognac imported was the brandy manufactured by Messrs *Sazerac-de-Forge et fils,* of Limoges, France. In 1859 the local importer of that brandy was John B. Schiller and in that year, when he opened at 13 Exchange Alley, he named his place the "Sazerac Coffee House" after the brand of cognac he served exclusively. Schiller's brandy cocktails became the drink of the moment and his business flourished. In 1870 his bookkeeper, Thomas H. Handy, succeeded as proprietor and the place became the "Sazerac House." A change in the mixture also took place. Peychaud's bitters continued to add just the right fillip. American rye whiskey was substituted for the French cognac. Although the brandy was eliminated the original name persisted, and the cocktail remains Sazerac to this day. For more details on local potables see the author's *Famous New Orleans Drinks and How to Mix 'Em.*

THE OLD GEM   127 ROYAL ST.

Just as one drink calls for another, so does one thirst-quenching emporium call for another description of an old building which gained its fame from the liquids and solids dispensed there in the old days. The Gem, erected and opened for business in 1851 by John Daniels and Alfred Arnold Pray, soon became very popular. On January 10, 1857, a number of New Orleans businessmen met in the rooms above the saloon and organized the *Mistick Krewe of Comus*, the first Carnival organization to give New Orleans a night street parade with floats. This organization meeting, four years before the outbreak of the Civil War, has been confused in the minds of some writers with the start of Carnival outdoor celebrations . . . the first street masking taking place in 1837 and not in 1857, as commonly and erroneously stated.

OLD MERCHANTS' EXCHANGE   126 ROYAL ST.

A flat, granite-faced building once occupied this address on the right-hand side of Royal Street and was the famous Merchants' Exchange during the golden boom days of New Orleans. Erected in 1835-36 at a cost of $100,000 from designs by Charles Bingley Dakin, the building fronted on both Royal Street and the *ruelle* or alley in the rear. This narrow thoroughfare was created in 1831 and, as the exchange was planned to have two entrances, the alley was named *Passage de la bourse* or Exchange Passage.

In 1842 the United States Post Office was established on the ground floor and a few years later the high-domed exchange room was occupied by the United States District Court. It was here that William Walker, colorful adventurer and former New Orleans newspaper editor, was tried for his filibustering operations against Nicaragua in 1856, where he made himself president and dictator.

After the Civil War, the old Merchants' Exchange was transformed into a sumptuous gambling palace where fortunes were made, but many more lost, by the turn of the card, the roll of the dice, or from wooing Dame Fortune at the shrines of lotto, keno, or roulette. Today the large room which once resounded with the calls of the trader, the auctioneer, the advocate pleading at the bar of justice, and the words of the keno dealer is gone. The Merchants' Exchange was destroyed by fire in the early 1960s.

OLD UNION BANK SITE   140 ROYAL ST.

On the upper right-hand corner of Royal and Iberville streets, adjoining the old Merchants' Exchange, is a modern drugstore. Until it was erected in 1948 this site was occupied by the Union Bank of Louisiana. Erected in 1832 the old bank building was planned by brother architects—Jacques Nicolas de Pouilly and Joseph Isadore de Pouilly, noted for the many handsome edifices they designed in old New Orleans.

LA LOUISIANE RESTAURANT   725 IBERVILLE ST.

As we arrive at Iberville Street on our journey along historic *rue Royale* there are few buildings worth our attention from an ancient viewpoint. Just before we cross the street we can glance to our left. Here is *Restaurant de la Louisiane,* which for many years has been the rendevous of those who demanded the ultimate in distinctive Creole cuisine.

The restaurant is housed in a one-time magnificently appointed residence that has known many owners of note. The structure dates back to 1834 when François Gardère, then state treasurer of Louisiana, purchased the site and structure from Mme Charlotte Livaudais, wife of Charles Papet, and evidently made extensive alterations, probably placing on the balconies the handsome cast-iron grillwork. The property passed to Dame Anne Duezan, widow of Jean Baptiste Riviere, who in 1836 sold the residence to James Waters Zacharie, a prominent commission merchant.

The adjoining structure towards Bourbon Street, in which are located La Louisiane's banqueting rooms, was built in 1832 by George Morgan and was owned from 1833 to 1870 by Judge Alonzo Morphy, father of Paul Morphy, the celebrated chess champion. The building between La Louisiane and the site of Solari's (corner of Iberville and Royal streets) was the old residence of Jacques Chalaron and is several years older than the structures just described.

Continuing down Royal Street we pass no building of historical importance until we arrive at the junction with Bienville. True, we do pass the Monteleone Hotel, the principal hostelry below Canal Street, and a number of antique shop display windows will capture our attention.

CONWAY'S COURT   240 ROYAL ST.

On the right-hand, upper corner of Royal and Bienville are two plastered-brick houses of considerable antiquity, known many years ago as "Conway's Court." They were built during the Spanish regime and previous to March 1799, for on the ninth of that month both were purchased from William Conway by a wealthy free woman of color named Fanchonette Robert. These two buildings, with their fine wrought-iron balcony railings, have not only defied the march of time but the march of progress as well. Alongside these ancient *casas* rise the towering stories of the Monteleone Hotel. No greater contrast of the very old with the very new is to be found anywhere else in the Vieux Carré.

MALLARD'S *MAGASIN*   301-305-307 ROYAL ST.

On the left-hand, downtown woods side of Royal and Bienville streets is a brick building with art galleries and an antique shop on the ground floor. Over a century ago a talented Frenchman had here his *magasin de meubles* where he carved out of mahogany, rosewood, walnut, and other lumber that came to his shop, the prized furniture that bears the name of Mallard.

Prudent Mallard, a native of Sèvres where he was born in 1809, learned his trade in Paris and came to New Orleans in the early 1830s. In 1838 he opened his own shop at old 292 Royal, between St. Philip and Ursulines streets. Gradually the products of his workshop found favor with the best folk and many came from plantation homes to purchase his four-poster beds, rosewood armoires, mahogany fireside chairs, and settees. In consequence he found it to his advantage to move "uptown" and in 1841 he was displaying his wares in the store at 305 Royal, while his workmen fabricated furniture in the corner building, and in these three structures carried on the business that brought him fame. Mallard's antiques command a high price today and are not easily secured.

To seekers of antique furniture distinctive of the old New Orleans craftsmen and wood-carvers, Mallard's name shines bright. Although François Seignouret holds top position, Prudent Mallard is a close second. Pierre Dutreuil Barjon and Henry N. Siebrecht, each talented, are other names revered by those seeking furniture manufactured in the Old Square.

The three buildings occupied by Mallard were erected in 1838 by Matthew Morgan, a New Orleans banker, and are typical of the architecture of the period that ushered in the "golden era" of old New Orleans.

The 300 block of Royal Street, between Bienville and Conti, is crowded with old buildings, typical structures of the combined business-home of the shopkeeper. The majority of them were erected during the period New Orleans was reveling in flush times. On the river side is a row of brick buildings erected by an English nobleman, the Earl of Balcanes, soon after he had purchased the sites in 1828 from a fellow countryman, Alexander Haliburton of Wigan. Many citizens of note occupied the combination store-and-residence buildings.

JOHN SLIDELL'S HOME   312 ROYAL ST.

This structure was owned and occupied by John Slidell in 1839. Slidell, an attorney of note who later became United States senator from Louisiana just prior to the Civil War, after hostilities began was appointed commissioner for the Confederacy to England. While on his way to his post he was taken from the British ship *Trent* by the commander of the USS *San Jacinto*. This act on the high seas became best known as the "Trent Affair," one that nearly brought the United States and Great Britain into conflict in 1861.

318-324 ROYAL STREET—This building, a little more pretentious than its fellows on that side of the street, was built shortly after Jacob Readel Wolff purchased the site from the Bank of Louisiana. One of the terms of the sale, made May 7, 1828, was that Wolff should erect a "modern three-story fireproof building." It has housed many important merchants in its ground-floor shops.

311 ROYAL STREET—Erected by François Durel in 1828, and for many years it housed "The Sign of the Magnolia." It was not a perfumery shop as you might suspect, but where C. Ludre had his boot and shoe store.

313-317 ROYAL STREET—A double or twin brick building erected in 1830 by Josephine Victoire Formosante Perrilliat, wife of C. B. Keeler, on the site of the old Perrilliat home. The erection cost was $14,800.

FIRST U.S. POST OFFICE   333 ROYAL ST.

Here was located the first United States Post Office to be established in New Orleans. In consequence old "23 *rue Royale*" was the center of interest following the arrival of the latest express. Mail in those days was carried overland by riders on horse, long before the pony express became famed in the annals of the West. Over the famed and dangerous Natchez Trace the express riders galloped through the Indian country, through Saint Francisville, Baton Rouge, Madisonville, and then by sailboat across Lake Pontchartrain. Or mail came via Mobile and the lake route to Bayou St. John. No matter the route, it was here that Postmaster Blaise Cenas sorted and delivered the folded and sealed missives to those who waited impatiently for them on the narrow *banquette*.

In the early 1840s a tenant of this old post office was a young French artist named Jules Lion, who brought with him from Paris a contrivance in picture making called a daguerreotype. It was from these daguerreotypes that M. Lion drew the lithographic likenesses of prominent New Orleanians who came to this studio and shop to sit for their portraits.

THE OLD GAZ BANK   339 ROYAL ST.

Before we reach the corner where Royal Street meets Conti, we should pause and look into the show windows of this nearly two-centuries-old building, for the arched pillars within support a structure that boasts an interesting history. It was erected in 1800, during the twilight of the Spanish domination, by Don Pablo Lanusse, senior judge of the *Illustrious Cabildo*. The building hummed with various activities in the years that followed and has the distinction of being the oldest structure in the Crescent City that has housed a bank.

This *casa grande* that Alcalde Lanusse erected is typical of the architecture of that period, and had in Royal Street a domed corridor leading to a spacious court, both of which have been bricked up in late years. Note the balcony railings of wrought iron, among the finest examples of Spanish craftsmanship to be found in the Vieux Carré. Like most of the early wrought iron on the balconies of the *Quartier*, the design is Moresque and doubtless the output of some Seville smithy and shipped overseas from Cadiz.

Corner balcony railing of wrought iron over the Old Gaz Bank

It is not known what manner of business was carried on in this building when it was erected but we do know that Thomas Elmes had his dry goods emporium here in 1805, and when he purchased it in 1807, the consideration was $33,000.

On May 2, 1811, *La Banque des Habitants*, "Planters' Bank" as we would say it, paid $50,000 for the structure and in the nine years that followed carried on its business here. On February 12, 1820, the Planters' Bank sold the property for $50,000 to the U.S. Bank of Philadelphia, which transferred its branch, located since 1805 at Chartres and Bienville streets, to this active business location.

Sixteen years later, on New Year's Day of 1836, the United States Bank sold the property for $50,000 to the New Orleans Gas Light & Banking Company, the last named concern moving to this corner from its original location in Magazine Street at Gravier, in the so-called "American" side of town. From that time the old Lanusse residence became known as the *Banque du Gaz* to the French-speaking folk or, with unconscious irony, "Gas Bank" to the English-speaking.

In October of 1838, following the banking panic of 1837 when virtually every bank in the city folded up and froze depositors' money, the Gaz bank was sold to Dr. Paul Lacroix for $75,000, who leased it to various commercial concerns.

OLD MORTGAGE OFFICE   334 ROYAL ST.

On the right-hand or river side of Royal Street at the corner of Conti, set in the center of a yard in which grow towering magnolia trees and enclosed by a very fine old iron fence, is a building with Ionic columns that has long been one of the old town's landmarks. Its age has been variously estimated but notarial acts show that

Old Louisiana Bank (drawn by Clarence Millet)

while the site was purchased on May 18, 1825, by the Bank of Louisiana from the heirs of Jean Noël d'Estrehan, the building was not erected until the winter of 1826-27. The architect was Benjamin F. Fox, and Tobias Bickle and Philip Hamblet were the contractors. Its erection cost the newly organized and second institution, to be called the Louisiana Bank, $80,000 exclusive of the sum paid for the site.

At the time of its erection and in the years that followed, Royal and Conti streets were the hub of the city's financial activities—three of its four corners having a bank. Unable to weather the stress of the Civil War, the bank was closed and in 1871 became "The Royal Street Auction Exchange." Realty operations were carried on in it until 1874 when Mayor L. A. Wiltz, acting for the city government, paid the bank's liquidators $12,800 for the site and structure, and possession has been retained by the city since that time. It became the Mortgage and Conveyance Office, and was best known to many old residents by the name of the "Old Mortgage Office."

Following World War I the old Bank of Louisiana became the home of the local American Legion and in 1935 underwent a number of interior and exterior repairs. Now the site is the New Orleans Police substation for the Vieux Carré.

LOUISIANA STATE BANK   401 ROYAL ST.

Before crossing Conti Street we should pause for a moment to survey the building on the lower left-hand corner of Royal and Conti streets. This imposing edifice—it deserves no other designation—was built in the latter part of 1821 to house the Louisiana State Bank, which accounts for the skillfully designed monogram *L S B* in the wrought-iron balcony railing on the Royal Street facade.

Countless visitors to the Vieux Carré have paused at this corner to admire the building's simple yet commanding proportions, the curving top of the side wall of Conti Street, and the entranceway that once admitted carriages to the charming courtyard, once one of the distinctive features of this property. Sad to relate, and view, this wall has been bricked up and a roof now covers that once-upon-a-time characteristic patio. Despite the fact that man has laid his desecrating hand on the courtyard he has not yet spoiled the beauty of the high walls of the main building nor its balcony ironwork, for the original wrought-iron decoration on the balconies is still there and just as it was hammered out on the anvils of the skilled ironmasters of nearly two centuries ago.

The site was owned in 1786 by Don Pedro Cenas but it was not until 1819 that his widow, Dame Marie Josephine Reine Cenas, sold the land to *La Banque de l'Etat de la Louisiane*, which was then transacting its business in the building that now houses Brennan's Restaurant. Soon after the purchase architects were invited to submit plans for a banking structure to occupy the corner, and on July 20, 1820, the design submitted by Benjamin Henry Boneval Latrobe was selected. Latrobe was the same skilled architect who had designed the south wing of the nation's capitol and who reconstructed it after its burning by the British forces in 1813. He had come to New Orleans in 1819 to superintend the construction of the city's waterworks begun by his son, Henry F. Boneval Latrobe.

Monogram of the Louisiana State Bank on the balcony railing

Although the elder Latrobe was the successful designer of the new bank, he did not live to see its erection. He fell a victim, as his son had, to yellow fever a few weeks after he had been adjudged the winner of the competition. Consequently, its construction was delayed, and when building operations were begun they were placed under the supervision of Benjamin F. Fox, a New Orleans constructor. The bank was opened for business just before Christmas 1821.

The Louisiana State Bank went on its way, as many another like institution, but it did hold the distinction of weathering most of the financial hurricanes that swept others out of business. Like many other Royal Street structures of note, the old bank building became a repository for relics from the homes of former Creole aristocrats. In 1916, a tenant named Leopold Levy, a dealer in old furniture and many other things ancient, renamed the Louisiana State Bank "The Antique Dome," an allusion to the construction of its interior, which is well worth viewing.

JEAN BLANQUE'S HOUSE   409 ROYAL ST.

Immediately adjoining the old Louisiana State Bank is a much older structure that for eight years was the town house of Jean Blanque, once a well-known figure in old New Orleans. He was a merchant, lawyer, banker, legislator, and—this was told in whispers—the "man higher up" in certain transactions relative to the importation of "black ivory" and goods upon which customs duty was not collected. M. Blanque earned this distinction during the hectic days before the Battle of New Orleans was fought, when the slave smuggling activities of a swaggering company of Baratarians under the leadership of Pierre and Jean Laffite, sometimes designated as pirates, were at their height. It will be remembered that it was to Jean Blanque that Jean Laffite sent his letters exposing the attempt of the British emissaries to seduce the Baratarians to the English cause prior to the appearance of the British invading army in 1815.

Jean Blanque was a native of Béarn, the old French province that now forms a part of the deparment of Basses-Pyrénées. He came to New Orleans on the frigate

Surveillant, March 26, 1803, with Pierre Clément de Laussat. He soon won a position of importance in his new home, and married Delphine Macarty, the widow of Don Ramon de Lopez y Angula. In the Blanque home in Royal Street were born four children, three daughters and a son, who played with Borquita, Delphine's daughter by her first marriage. Jean Blanque's wife, it might be now pointed out, became best known in New Orleans history as "Madame Lalaurie," the mistress of the so-called "Haunted House" at 1140 Royal Street.

This Royal Street mansion in which the Blanques entertained lavishly was not built by Jean Blanque. He purchased it from François Marie Godefroy du Jarreau, an architect and builder, who erected it and the adjoining mansion in 1807.

THE ROUQUETTE HOME   413 ROYAL ST.

This building in days long gone by was the home of a number of families whose names are prominent in Louisiana's colorful history. On the wrought-iron balcony railing above the entrance to this fine old house is fashioned the monogram *D R,* the initials of Dominique Rouquette who purchased the building in 1809, two years after its erection by architect du Jarreau, who had also constructed the old Blanque mansion.

Dominique Rouquette came to New Orleans in 1800 from Bordeaux, France, became a merchant and importer of wines from his native province and, as the wine business furnished lucrative returns, in a short time he became quite wealthy. Marrying Louise Cousin, a family of four boys and one daughter blessed the union and one of the sons born beneath this roof on February 26, 1813, became a beloved figure in the world of letters and the priesthood. He was Adrien Rouquette, better known by his Choctaw Indian name, *Chahta-Ima.*

After receiving an excellent education in the schools of Kentucky and Pennsylvania, Adrien Rouquette was sent to Paris to round out his education. Upon his return to his native state he sought the seclusion of the green forests of Saint Tammany Parish, across Lake Pontchartrain. In the Bayou Lacombe region he mingled

with the Choctaw Indians and there fell in love with a chief's daughter. She was *Oushola*, in the Indian tongue "Bird Singer." Adrien took unto himself an Indian name, *Chahta-Ima*, meaning "Like a Choctaw." After the death of his sweetheart young Rouquette forsook the redmen, returned to New Orleans, and then went to Paris to study law.

In France he turned his talents to writing and from his pen came many prose poems. Although his writings were extravagantly praised he threw aside all desire for writing and returned once more to Louisiana. Back in his native city he suddenly decided to take on holy orders so he might become a missionary among the Choctaws. With the Indians he entered on a life of self-denial and by his devotion secured many converts to his religion. Abbé Rouquette's name will live long—as long, so it is hoped, as his father's initials in the wrought-iron railing of his Royal Street birthplace.

BRENNAN'S RESTAURANT   417 ROYAL ST.

Unquestionably one of the most interesting buildings in the Vieux Carré is that structure directly opposite the main entrance of the New Orleans Court Building, which for many years housed a restaurant known as the Patio Royal. Of undoubted antiquity, its genesis has long been a matter of conjecture. Various estimates have been made as to its age, the identity of the man who built it, the uses to which it was put before housing Louisiana's first banking institution, and other information dear to the confirmed student of antiquity and architecture. Only recent research has established authentic data regarding its early history. The handsome structure was erected during the twilight of Spanish rule over Louisiana by Don José Faurie, a wealthy merchant of that period, on a site long owned by Don Vicente Rillieux. Aged and dog-eared Spanish notarial acts inform us that after her husband's death Dame Maria Fronquet Rillieux made over the *terreno* to Santiago Freret, who had married her daughter Eugenie, and that on June 2, 1801, James Freret relinquished title to the site to Señor Faurie for 8,650 hard Mexican *pesos*. It was subsequent to this sale that the new owner erected the present mansion. He made it his combination residence and place of business until January 26, 1805, when

© M.M. Hobbs. PATIO ROYAL   OLD NEW ORLEANS

Cast-iron plaque with monogram of Louisiana Bank

Julien Poydras, as president of the newly organized *Banque de la Louisiane,* paid Señor Faurie $25,000 for the land and structure. This Louisiana Bank, first banking institution to be operated in New Orleans and the vast territory secured by the United States through the Louisiana Purchase, was created March 11, 1804, by Governor W. C. C. Claiborne.

To fit it for banking purposes, the Faurie mansion underwent a few changes. Those worth noticing were the wrought-iron decorations on the balconies that jutted over the Royal Street *banquette.* The supporting brackets under the central balcony are interesting examples of the *ferronniers'* art, quite as interesting and compelling to architects and ironworkers as the railing that edges the *mirador,* as the Spanish named these balconies. At each end of this balcony railing can be seen the graceful *L B* monogram enclosed in an octagon, while in the center of the front railing the Louisiana Bank's initials are embossed on a solid iron plaque, around which twine two snakes (strange design this, for a bank!), and a pair of cornucopias. Those two horns of Amalthaea, it will be noticed, are spewing a flood of coins—a still stranger design for a bank!

In 1819, after the original Louisiana Bank had outlived its chartered life, its ground-floor quarters were occupied by the Louisiana State Bank, just then being organized, until its own building at the corner of Conti Street could be erected from Latrobe's plans. On October 5, 1820, the liquidators of *La Banque de la Louisiane* sold the property to Martin Gordon, clerk of the United States District Court, a cultured gentleman from Virginia and very prominent socially.

The Gordon family made their home in the apartment above and dispensed a sumptuous and lavish hospitality. Consequently, it soon became the center of stylish Creole social activities. Martin Gordon was prominent in the hot politics of the day, and in 1828, when General Jackson revisited the city he saved fro: 1 the British invaders, the hero of Chalmette was the guest of Martin Gordon, who gave here banquet after banquet in honor of the distinguished visitor. His host's hospitality was not forgotten when "Old Hickory" took up his residence in the White

House, for Martin Gordon became collector of the port of New Orleans, a prized office in those days.

In 1841 Martin Gordon and his son met with financial reverses and the fine old *casa*, that Joseph Faurie had built with great pride forty years before, was seized by the Citizen's Bank and sold at auction by the sheriff. The purchaser was Judge Alonzo Morphy, whose $34,900 proved to be high bid. In spite of the fact that he was a prominent member of the bar, had been state attorney general, and one of the members of Louisiana's high court, Judge Morphy's greater fame now hinges on the fact that he was the father of Paul Charles Morphy, the celebrated American chess master.

Although not born in this Royal Street house, it was here that little ten-year-old Paul learned the moves in the intricate game and before he was in his teens the youngster was worsting the best New Orleans chess players . . . and they were legion in those days. When he was just of age, Paul Morphy was in England and France, defeating Europe's foremost chess champions—even playing eight contestants at one time while blindfolded. This New Orleans-born wizard with kings, queens, bishops, and rooks was born June 27, 1837, in an ancient building still standing at 1113 Chartres Street, opposite the original Ursulines' convent, in a home erected by his grandfather Joseph LeCarpentier. The Chess King died in this Royal Street mansion in 1884. He had studied law but, oversmart, had become "a gentle witling" and at the age of forty-seven passed away while taking a bath on a hot day. Two years later his brothers and sisters sold the mansion.

The name of the Morphy family was originally Irish . . . Omurphy. It became in time O'Murphy, then Murphy and, when an ancestor fled Ireland because of religious persecution and went to Spain, it became, finally, Morphy. It was Don Diego Morphy, a native of Madrid, who brought this distinguished name to New Orleans in 1803.

In 1920 title to this ancient and historically important property passed to Tulane University through the generosity of William Ratcliffe Irby, who made his fortune in tobacco, and when a distinctive French Quarter restaurant was opened here, the old Faurie-Gordon-Morphy mansion was rechristened with the fanciful name "Patio Royal." Brennan's Restaurant now occupies the building.

NEW ORLEANS COURT BUILDING   400 ROYAL ST.

Directly across the street, on the river or right-hand side of the street, and occupying the entire square bounded by Royal, Conti, Chartres, and St. Louis streets, is the building that housed many state and city departments, including the Supreme Court, Court of Appeals, Civil District and City Courts, Department of Conservation, Mortgage, Conveyance, and the Notarial Offices where were stored the priceless and authentic records of real estate transactions of the past—those that were painstakingly searched in the preparation of this history of the Vieux Carré.

Erected in 1910 at a cost of a million dollars, it is, properly, the New Orleans Court Building—not the "New Courthouse Building" as it was usually, and incorrectly, designated even by those housed in it.

The Supreme Court moved from this imposing building to new quarters on Loyola Avenue in the late 1950s. The Fifth Circuit Court of Appeals relocated to a new Central Business District courthouse in the 1970s, and all of the other city offices have found new homes in a civic complex on Loyola Avenue. During the 1970s and early 1980s, the old courthouse offices were used by the Louisiana Department of Wildlife and Fisheries.

For many years a bronze figure in judicial robes stood on the granite steps leading to the entrance. This statue of Edward Douglas White, distinguished jurist, native of Louisiana, and former chief justice of the United States Supreme Court, now stands in Duncan Plaza next to the Louisiana Supreme Court Building.

THE COCKTAIL IS BORN   437 ROYAL ST.

This antique shop, not differing a great deal from the many such establishments found today in almost every block of the ancient thoroughfare, holds an interest not usually the fortune of the regular run of old furniture and trinket places . . . for here was conceived and born that peculiar and throat-satisfying liquid concoction, the American cocktail. Here, too, so a well-authenticated tradition informs us, was this popular drink given its name.

The notarial acts consulted inform us that this building, and its corner twin, was erected in 1800 by Don José Pavis, and that, in 1816 Nicolas Girod, the mayor of New Orleans, purchased the property for $32,000. Be that as it may, our interest lies in its first tenant—a native of Santo Domingo, forced to flee that island by the uprising of the blacks in 1795, who here opened a successful and popular drugstore. The apothecary's name was Antoine Amédée Peychaud, one of the *Dominguois* who flocked to Spanish Louisiana when the blacks drove them from their island in the sunlit Caribbean.

New Orleans owes much to these French-speaking islanders. To them are due the first newspaper in Louisiana, the first theatre, and the cultivation of sugarcane. To these white *Dominguois* is also due the word "*Créole*," which we use to distinguish the native Louisianian of French or Spanish descent. The word was originally Spanish, *criollo*, to bring up or rear, and applied only to the descendants of Spanish colonists born in the New World, but the use of the term spread to the French West Indies, and was brought to New Orleans by the refugees from Santo Domingo. To the above roster of boons given Louisiana by the *Dominguois* we now must add the word "cocktail."

A. A. Peychaud's bid for fame and popularity was not founded so much upon the quality of the drugs he dispensed over the counter of his apothecary shop, but in the bitters he compounded and concocted from a secret formula he brought with him from his native island. These bitters, good for what ailed you irrespective of the malady, gave an added zest to the potions of cognac brandy he served his cronies in the pharmacy after meetings of his Masonic Lodge. Peychaud was W. M. of Concorde Blue Lodge, Grand Orator of the Grand Lodge, High Priest of the Royal Arch, and belonged to other divisions of that fraternity, for he was a "joiner." The fame of this highly flavored dram of brandy served by the *Pharmacie Peychaud* spread and the place became a popular rendezvous.

Peychaud had a unique way of preparing his concoction using the old-fashioned double-ended egg-cup as a measuring cup—what we now call the jigger. The French-speaking folk of old New Orleans knew this piece of table crockery as a *coquetier* (pronounced *ko-k-tay'*), and those who could not properly pronounce French called the libation a "cocktay," or possibly, through sampling too many of M. Peychaud's spiced brandies, the English-speaking were soon designating them "cocktails."

We can interrupt our saunter down *rue Royale* for a moment or two and deserting it turn into the street named for Louis, the patron saint of France.

CONAND MANSION   722 ST. LOUIS ST.

One of the once-upon-a-time typical mansions of the Vieux Carré, rescued from decay and neglect within late years, is the old Conand home in St. Louis Street. The old mansion has a handsome and beflowered courtyard but, unfortunately for the tourist who delights in exploring such typical patios, this private residence is not thrown open to the many from far away who throng the French Quarter in the winter months, so we must content ourselves with a tantalizing glimpse of the court through the gateway grille.

As far back as 1787 this site was the property of Don Pedro Hébert for on August 9 of that year, ancient notarial records tell us, he sold the ground to Don Mathias Francisco de Alpuente, who had come to the Louisiana colony with the Spanish governor O'Reilly. In 1808 his property was divided and sold by his widow. On the site of the old Alpuente one-story *casa* the purchaser of the site, Dr. Joseph Conand, a prominent physician, erected the present mansion that year.

ANTOINE'S   713 ST. LOUIS ST.

Before we retrace our steps, to again take up our sight-seeing saunter along Royal Street, we can pause for a moment to glance across the street and survey the building that houses the most famous and oldest restaurant in the Vieux Carré—Antoine's.

Since 1862 the given name of Antoine Alciatore has been synonymous with many characteristic and delectable dishes that have made old and new New Orleans cookery famous. A few years earlier Alciatore left his native France to gain fame and fortune, which he found in the Franco-American city on the banks of the Mississippi River. Naturally, a young and penniless Frenchman and his wife began their culinary conquest of the city of their selection in a modest way—standing before a hot stove creating dishes that make gourmets inclined to enshrine chefs as saints.

The building that now houses the original Antoine's was erected as a residence by James Ramsey, himself a builder of note, and after passing through various ownerships, was purchased by Antoine Alciatore from the Miltenberger family on August 20, 1868.

GRANDCHAMPS' *PHARMACIE*   501 ROYAL ST.

The building at the northwest corner of Royal and St. Louis is noteworthy because of the lacework of cast iron that completely encloses its second-story balcony which fronts the two streets. Built in 1806 by Charles Baromée Dufau, the place was occupied from 1809 by François Grandchamps, whose celebrated pharmacy was located on the ground-floor corner shop. In 1821, soon after Grandchamps purchased the building for $14,000, he had as a tenant in the apartments above the drugstore John Vanderlyn, noted American portrait painter. Vanderlyn's studio became a popular social rendezvous while the artist was brushing on canvas the likenesses of wealthy Orleanians, planters from cotton-growing sections, and their wives and daughters. It was here, too, that the excitable and talented bird artist, John James Audubon, had his seriocomic encounter with the portrait painter.

WIDOW ROCHE'S RESIDENCE   505 ROYAL ST.

One of the distinctive yet unobtrusive buildings of the French Quarter is the old home of Widow Roche. It has a small but characteristic court at the end of the arched corridor, barred at the inner end by a handsome wrought-iron gate.

The history of this old mansion begins with the purchase of the site, which included the corner lot, by Charles Baromée Dufau from Antoine Peytavin Reynaud in 1806, and it was Dufau, apparently, who erected this and the Grandchamps building.

SAINT LOUIS HOTEL SITE/
ROYAL ORLEANS HOTEL   ROYAL AND ST. LOUIS STS.

On this spot once rose in all its magnificence the Saint Louis Hotel, one of the most famous hostelries in the United States, a monument to the early wealth, elegance, and prosperity of New Orleans during its golden boom days.

Construction began in 1835 at a cost of $1.5 million from designs by two talented Frenchmen, Jacques Nicolas de Pouilly, and his brother, Joseph Isadore de Pouilly. Completed in 1838, the new hotel was named for the patron saint of the city and it became at once the popular resort of the wealthy sugar planters and slave owners. It also housed the city's auction exchange, brilliantly illuminated ballrooms, dining salons, and, on the Royal Street side, was the slave block which became celebrated in song and story. Pierre Maspero was the first manager but in 1839 the management of the hotel was leased to Pierre Rudolph Marty, the "R. Marty" who had made the old Planters & Strangers' Hotel in Chartres Street a popular success as early as 1812.

A fire in 1841 gutted the handsome original structure but another palace immediately replaced the first hotel which, under the design of Isadore de Pouilly, took on the architectural splendor of the predecessor. In time this building, which took up the entire St. Louis Street front from Royal to Chartres, duplicated the popularity of the original hotel. It was renamed Hotel Royal but gradually fell into neglect and decay and, after being unoccupied for years, a hurricane in 1915 tore off its roof. Declared a public menace, a wrecking crew razed what time and wind failed to accomplish, and the Vieux Carré lost a spectacular antique that could have been easily and inexpensively preserved for posterity.

The cleared site was used as a parking lot for many years until the Royal Orleans Hotel was built in 1960. A painting in the lobby of this new hotel, executed by New Orleans artist Boyd Cruise, beautifully illustrates the fascinating history of the old Saint Louis Hotel.

MAISON SEIGNOURET   520 ROYAL ST.

Next to the Saint Louis Hotel site is one of the finest structures in the Old Square. Its court is famed because of the many pictures that have been made of it by painters, etchers, and photographers. The building is now occupied by the broadcasting studios of WDSU and WDSU-TV.

This splendid mansion was erected in 1816 by a native of Bordeaux, France, who came to New Orleans prior to the day he shouldered a musket as a member of the *Bataillon d'Orléans* to aid General Jackson in hurling back the British invading forces on the fields of Chalmette. In coming back to *Nouvelle-Orléans,* it was this Frenchman's prime intention to import the extract of the grape from his native province and thus satisfy the discriminating palates of the Creoles. They had been forced for a third of a century to swallow *"le poison de Catalogne"* by the late Spanish

Patio of Maison Seignouret (etching by Knute Heldner)

Corner of courtyard of Maison Seignouret,
520 Royal St., built in 1816
(drawn and copyrighted by Morris Henry Hobbs)

masters, whereas Creole palates had been educated and throats fashioned by nature for the mellowed sweetness of *le vin de Bordeaux!*

This importer was François Seignouret, who throughout his business career in old New Orleans distributed wines of the highest quality for the elite. His name today, however, is not revered for the wines from Bordeaux, the fiery cognac from Charente, nor the smooth vermouth from Marseilles that he sold from his veritable palace . . . he is best known for the furniture he designed and manufactured at old 64, 116, or 144, for old *rue Royale* was a street of changing numbers before 1871. In the workshops off the pleasant courtyard skilled artisans, under the watchful eye of the master, fabricated the dainty tables, tabourets, chaise longues, fragile chairs, massive armoires—the "Seignourets" so prized by discriminating collectors of antiques.

A noticeable construction of the building is the *entresol,* or mezzanine, a half-story just above the ground floor. Here it was that the wine merchant stored his *barils,* pipes, and casks of precious ruby-red liquids. The wrought-iron work on the long balcony of the third story which juts over the Royal Street *banquette* is of exquisite design. Especially noteworthy is the guard screen, or *garde de frise,* a fan-shaped affair excellently designed to keep possible marauders from passing from one adjoining balcony to another. One should not neglect noting the *S* hammered into the *garde de frise,* for many have claimed that all of Seignouret's furniture had his initial letter incorporated somewhere in the design.

The courtyard, unquestionably one of the best known in the Vieux Carré, is a beautiful patio where for a number of years the New Orleans Arts and Crafts Club had a school for aspiring art students.

Seignouret carried on his combination winery and furniture importing and manufacturing business until his death, which occured in his native France. In 1856 his widow and children sold the property to Emile Seignouret, his brother, and in this same mansion, under the name of E. Seignouret & Charles Cavaroc, was carried on the business which made the name Seignouret famous in old New Orleans. Pierre Ernest Brulatour rented the building in 1870 and carried on his wine importing business here until 1886, and for that reason the *Maison Seignouret* is sometimes called the Brulatour building. In 1900 William Ratcliffe Irby, wealthy tobacco manufacturer and philanthropist, became owner of the house that François Seignouret built.

Adjoining the Seignouret home are three three-story buildings on the right-hand side of Royal, bearing the numbers 528-530-532, which were erected in 1828 by Hart Moses Schiff.

MAISON DE COMMERCE 534 ROYAL ST.

It is the building next but one to the corner of Toulouse Street that we may inspect from the point of antiquity and historical interest. Of characteristic Spanish-Creole construction, as the arched corridor, cypress *porte cochère,* and *entresol* testify, the exact date of its erection is not known but it was not standing after the fire of

December 1794, for that conflagration reduced the buildings in this section of the city to heaps of glowing embers.

Our earliest record, that of October 1, 1804, proves Fouque purchased this and an adjoining *magasin* from the creditors of Lille Sarpy & Cortes, the main structure being called "*Maison de Commerce.*" Jean Baptiste Lille Sarpy and his partner Juan Cortes, a Mexican merchant, carried on, during the closing days of the Spanish regime, an extensive merchandising business in this house and the adjoining *almacén,* which was torn down in 1828.

"SPANISH *COMANDANCIA*"   519 ROYAL ST.

This interesting yet unobtrusive two-story building of plastered brick has long been pointed out as the "old Spanish *Comandancia.*" Here, according to hoary tradition, the mounted police quartered their horses when Don Esteban Miro was governor at the time the red and yellow banner of Spain waved over the *Plaza de Armas.* As a matter of fact these headquarters were near the government house at Toulouse Street and the Mississippi River and not in this building, tradition to the contrary notwithstanding.

The building's facade gives no hint of its massiveness for the ancient brick walls extend deep into the rear of the lot. A side driveway, barred by an iron gate, is flanked by two half-buried upended cannons and lends a martial aspect to the place. While this old structure has a history that seemed to prove it to have been existing and doing business as long ago as 1774, the building here was burned to the ground in the fire of December 1794. We learn from a series of age-yellowed notarial acts that this was once the site of the commercial establishment of Don Jacob Cowperthwait, admittedly a queer name for a Spaniard, and that he was in business here for years. When his succession was opened the business and property were sold to Don Antonio Peytavin, who carried on the commercial business through the closing years of the Spanish rule over Louisiana. Here was sold the "fish oil" used to illuminate the street lanterns in the nights of the rule of the Dons. This illuminant was Nantucket whale oil.

Two years after the American occupation, the place was purchased by a firm of merchants, Samuel Winter and Thomas L. Harmon, who here conducted their trading business, only to sell the business in 1805 to a firm of Boston merchants, Nathaniel Amory and Thomas Callender. Twenty years later Amory & Callender took William Nott into their firm and the place was operated as William Nott & Company. In 1828, when the business was sold to Joseph Abat, the deed of sale stated that two of the three brick rear warehouses "had been built recently." The front building was probably erected in 1805.

CASA MERIEULT/
THE HISTORIC NEW ORLEANS COLLECTION   527-529-533 ROYAL ST.

One of the substantial old-timers lining ancient and romantic Royal Street is *Casa* Merieult. It was built in 1792 and we can authoritatively point it out as one of the

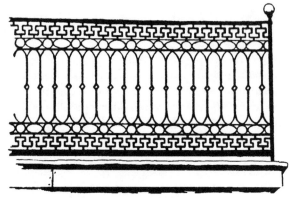

Detail of the cast-iron balcony railing at 529 Royal St.

two principal structures in the heart of old New Orleans which escaped being consumed in the disastrous fire of December 8, 1794.

The builder was Jean François Merieult (if you have difficulty with his name pronounce it "Mary-oo"), a Frenchman who came to New Orleans from Normandy when the Louisiana province was dominated by Spain. On November 16, 1791, he married Catherine Marguerite Macnamara, known to her intimates as "Damcees" and noted, in this city of raven-haired beauties, because her crowning glory was a magnificent mass of golden hair. As her father was Patrick Macnamara this probably accounts for its unusual color, but it does not tell us why he liked to be known as "Count" Macnamara. Catherine's mother, Judith Marguerite Chavin de Lery des Islets, however, was Creole-French to her fingertips and a member of a distinguished early Louisiana family.

When Catherine Macnamara became the wife of Jean Merieult the golden-haired Creole girl plighted her troth to a man who, aside from being a successful importer, became a junior judge or *alcalde* in the *Illustrious Cabildo,* the Spanish governing body of *Nueva Orleans.* In the following spring, when the succession of Don Pedro Arragon y Villigas was opened and his property in *Calle Real* offered for sale on April 25, 1792, Merieult purchased this site for 1,610 *pesos* and on it built this *Casa de Comercio.* Here it was, in the apartments above his business rooms, that *Alcalde Juan Francisco Merieult* settled with his bride and here were born their three children, Catherine Mathilde, Charles, and Euphrosine.

When Merieult, then a citizen of the United States, went to France on business connected with his vast shipping, importing, and exporting activities, with him went his handsome blonde wife. In Paris she attracted considerable attention aside from the fact she was the beautiful wife of a rich American because of her high-piled mass hair—so long and thick and so resembling the color of burnished gold. So was born one of the exciting traditions of old New Orleans—how the tresses of this handsome head of hair, worth more than a castle in France, came near to adorning the head of a favorite in the harem of the Sultan of Turkey.

At the time the Merieults were in Paris, Napoleon Bonaparte, then emperor of the French and aspiring to become master of the world, was anxious to secure a political alliance with Turkey. So, when it was reported to him that the sultan wanted a blonde wig for one of his sultanas, Napoleon decided to secure one for him. He was unsuccessful in this quest until his empress, Josephine, informed him her hairdresser had told her that he had been attending a lady from America who possessed a *chevelure* of the kind desired by the emperor but, as the lady was high-born and rich, she would probably not want to part with it. Napoleon, so the story goes, sent an aide to the fair Louisianian to ascertain how much gold she wanted in exchange for her gold hair. Offer on top of offer was made by the emperor until finally a castle was proffered. To each and every offer Damcees Macnamara-Merieult returned a decisive "No!" Although she lost a castle, she retained the most sought-after head of hair in France, and compelled a sultana to do without a coveted *perruque d'or.*

The cast-iron railing on a balcony which runs the width of the Royal Street facade of *Casa Merieult* is a particularly fine example of the ironmasters' art and is not duplicated anywhere in the Old Square. Many mistake it for wrought iron.

Ownership of *Casa* Merieult did not change until 1819, when the widow sold the place for $37,050. In 1938, General and Mrs. L. Kemper Williams purchased the Merieult house at the suggestion of architect Richard Koch, a pioneer preser-vationist who directed the Historic American Building Survey in New Orleans. Under Koch's direction, the building was extensively repaired, and it continued to serve both commercial and residential purposes.

The Williamses were collectors of books, maps, paintings, papers, and other ar-tifacts documenting Louisiana history. In 1974 the Merieult house was opened to the public as the Historic New Orleans Collection, a museum and research center housing the materials collected by General and Mrs. Williams.

COURT OF THE TWO LIONS   541 ROYAL ST.

This venerable corner building has long been popular with tourists, especially with visiting artists, because the courtyard on the Toulouse Street side is guarded by two crouching lions atop the gate posts. It is best known by the popular name "Court of the Two Lions." Although both lions have manes, the sculptor made sure that one would be recognized as a male and the other a lioness.

The structure has had an ancient and honorable career. "The Court of the Two Lions" was built in the latter part of 1798 by Jean François Merieult soon after he acquired the site by two purchases, the corner and Royal Street side from Jean Bap-tiste Poeyfarré, July 10, 1796, and the Toulouse Street side from Felix de Materre, July 5, 1798. The building became Alcalde Merieult's *Casa de Comercio* and when his widow sold the place on April 28, 1819, the purchaser was Vincent Nolte, the German merchant whose autobiographical *Fifty Years in Both Hemispheres* proved so useful to Hervey Allen when this modern author was confecting his elephantine historical novel, *Anthony Adverse.*

It was in this corner building that Vincent Nolte carried on his commission busi-ness for eight years before selling the place, in 1827, to *La Banque de l'Association,* successor to the original *Banque des Habitants de la Louisiane,* or as we would shorten

Court of the Two Lions (drawn by George Pierce)

it, the Planters' Bank. For five years, or until its final liquidation, the consolidated association of planters here carried on their business of loaning money to sugar planters. In 1832 the liquidators sold the building to the Havana commission firm of Lizardi Hermanos, the Cuban brothers composing the firm being Miguel, Francisco, and Manuel Lizardi. *El Patio de los Dos Leones* (or as the French-speaking Creoles named it, *La Cour des Lions*) has known many owners and various kinds of business have been carried on in its ground-floor shops.

The Toulouse Street courtyard, which gained its name and fame from the two marble lions *couchants* on the gate posts, has long attracted every artist of pen, brush, pencil, and etching needle visiting the Vieux Carré. Nor have writers of historical fiction failed to notice them. Winston Churchill in his *Crossing* described the patio and named it as the residence of his heroine. According to some accounts, the lions were not originally a decoration for the gate posts but were first used on the steps of the old Citizens' Bank of Louisiana located in the 600 block of Toulouse Street, for many years a picturesque ruin before it was demolished.

DREUX MANSION   714 TOULOUSE ST.

Adjoining the "Court of the Two Lions" is the old home, built in 1835, of Guy Dreux, a descendant of one of the original settlers of the city. Guy Dreux it was who maintained a brickyard in the section we now call Gentilly, a corruption of *Chantilly*, the original naming of that part of the city. From the Dreux brick kilns came many of the bricks that are now a part of the walls of many ancient buildings of the Old Square. The house is now a part of the Historic New Orleans Collection museum complex.

BAKER D'AQUIN'S HOME   720-722 TOULOUSE ST.

This is the old home of Louis d'Aquin, a well-known baker of bread in this old town. It was built prior to September 11, 1805, for on that date Jean Baptiste Soraparu became the owner of the ancient Spanish *casa*, which he only held a year. In 1806 Dame Adelaide Segond, the widow of James Carrick, purchased the old mansion and made it her home.

During the winter of 1938 and the early spring of 1939, playwright Tennessee Williams lived in the rooming house which then occupied this building. Williams later used the months of his stay on Toulouse Street as the basis for his play *Vieux Carré*, in which he specifically set the scene of the action "in a rooming house, 722 Toulouse Street." The building now houses the Manuscripts Division of the Historic New Orleans Collection.

On the opposite side of Toulouse Street are three ancient landmarks, a trio of buildings built during the latter part of the Spanish regime.

727-729 TOULOUSE ST.—The building nearest Bourbon Street was at one time the residence of A. A. Peychaud, the druggist who gave Americans that distinctive and palate-pleasing liquid refreshment—the cocktail. The building in which the originator of the cocktail lived was erected by Jean Baptiste Lille Sarpy in 1800. The building is now the Hôtel Maison de Ville.

CASA FLINARD   723 TOULOUSE ST.

This was the *casa grande* of Don Gerome Flinard in 1802, but further delving into the mystery of time and the erection of ancient structures in the Vieux Carré tells us little more than on October 27 of that year, Señor Flinard sold the place to Santiago Lemelle. Five years later the Widow Lemelle willed the property to Marguerite Boisdoré, wife of Valery Nicolas, a cordwainer, for by such a name was a shoemaker known here in the old, old days. As the Valery Nicolas mansion it was known until 1828. Since that time a number of citizens of old New Orleans have called the old Flinard place home. It has a courtyard worth visiting, reached through a typical domed corridor, and can well be considered a showplace. The place has been restored.

717 TOULOUSE ST.—This three-story brick structure appears to be the first tenement or apartment building erected in the Old Square. The builder was Jacques P. Meffre-Rouzan, son of a prominent East Baton Rouge planter.

HOME OF MADELINE BIZOT   719-721 TOULOUSE ST.

The one-story plastered-brick building, with a double-dip roof which stamps it at once as belonging to the Spanish period, is one of the venerable ancients among the many old residences in the heart of the city. The earliest record concerning it is to be found in the written acts of Don Esteban de Quinones, a notary in the days of the rule of the Dons. On June 21, 1799, so the yellowed pages scrawled with quaint ink scratches from the notary's crow quill tell us, Madeline Bizot, a *femme de couleur libre*, acquired the house and lot from Don José Bigot. When Señor Bigot built the place the notary did not deem it of sufficient importance to incorporate in the act of sale.

Although we must now return to Royal Street we will not turn down it until we have inspected several other Toulouse Street buildings on the river side of *rue Royale*.

MAISON JACOB   628 TOULOUSE ST.

Why this fine old structure, a mansion typical of the Spanish-Creole builders of old New Orleans, should have become designated by tradition as the one-time residence of William Charles Cole Claiborne, the first American governor of Louisiana, is one of the Old Square's best mysteries.

Ancient notarial acts fail to show that Governor Claiborne ever owned this once-upon-a-time elegant residence although they do prove that while he governed the state and the city he lived at the old government house at Old Levée (now Decatur) and Toulouse streets. There is no mystery shrouding the identity of the early owners of the site nor the name of the man who built the mansion and lived in it two years after Claiborne's death. This builder was Jean François Jacob, a wealthy planter of Saint John the Baptist Parish, who made it his town house for sixteen years.

M. Jacob, on September 7, 1813, set about erecting on the site a suitable town house for himself and his wife, Victoire Jourdan, also of a distinguished Louisiana family. What it cost to build this once imposing structure is not known but when M. Jacob sold it in 1819 Demoiselle Julie Robert Avart paid him $27,000 for it and she lived there until the day of her death in 1858.

During the 1930s and 1940s, the old Jacob mansion became the abode of artists, many of whom delighted in placing on canvas or etching in copper many of the old and distinguished homes of the Quarter. The immense fan window that looks out upon the courtyard is probably the most photographed, etched, and painted fan window in New Orleans . . . and there are many in the Vieux Carré.

On the lower side of Toulouse Street, between Chartres and Royal, facing the old Jacob mansion, is a row of old houses which were occupied by many of the aristocrats of the Hispanic-Franco and early American periods. We can glance at them before we return to Royal Street to continue our sight-seeing jaunt down the old thoroughfare.

619-621 TOULOUSE ST.—This was at one time the combination residence and commercial house of Robert Avart, a prominent planter and merchant, and the

Creole fan window overlooking the patio of Maison Jacob, 628 Toulouse St.
Probably the most photographed and painted window in old New Orleans
(drawn and copyrighted by Morris Henry Hobbs)

This self-supporting stairway long admired by artists,
architects, and photographers is at 623 Toulouse St.

date of its erection is only conjectural. In 1817 the tenant was none other than Vincent Nolte, the German merchant whose autobiographical *Fifty Years in Both Hemispheres* supplied Hervey Allen with most of the material for his thick and popular book *Anthony Adverse.*

623 TOULOUSE ST.—This residence was the home of Jean Antoine Demarchy, a well-known builder of the early days. When he erected it in 1807, after purchasing the site from Jayme Jorda, he exercised his talents in designing the structure—the most noteworthy feature being the twisting stairway from the rear of the corridor which takes one to the second-story apartments. Artists, architects, and photographers have long admired the window that looks out upon the courtyard, and the fanlight above it.

629 and 631 TOULOUSE ST.—These twin brick buildings were erected in 1838 by Henry Perret and Amable Charbonnet, a firm of commission merchants, and are in a better state of preservation than the house at 623 Toulouse. The builders purchased the site from Dame Charlotte Constance Hélène Jorda, the widow of Nicolas Reggio, member of a prominent Spanish family. Each has fine stairways leading to the floors above, which have been strikingly pictured by photographers.

COURT OF THE THREE ARCHES   600-604-606-608 ROYAL ST.

Just before we reach Royal Street we should cross Toulouse so we may look into the patio of a rambling two-story building on the northeast corner of these two streets. "The Court of the Three Arches" was the name given this small patio by some poet in recognition of the trio of brick pillars that support the main structure and separates it from the old three-story cuisine and slave quarters in the rear. Note that the balconies of the old slave quarters are lined with what appear to be the original cypress railings.

For nearly a quarter of a century this was the home and mercantile establishment of Dr. Germain Ducatel. Ten years after he fought under "Old Hickory" at the Battle of New Orleans, the physician abandoned his profession and contracted with Benjamin F. Fox, designer of many other now historic buildings in the Old Square, to build the present building on the foundations of the old town home of Rudolph Joseph Ducros, which extends along Royal Street.

When the building was finished in 1825 and the contractors paid their well-earned $12,066, Dr. Ducatel opened his *Magasin de Nouveautés* in the corner ground-floor store and this dry goods emporium was one of the most popular of its kind in the old city.

THE BRIGOT BUILDINGS   601-605-607 ROYAL ST.

The triple brick building on the downtown woods corner of Royal and Toulouse streets, and directly opposite the Court of the Three Arches, for a century housed many prominent Creole families in the upper apartments while in the ground-floor shops many important and quaint Creole characters carried on their business affairs.

Spanish wrought iron dating from 1800, at 339 Royal St.

The owner was Nicolas Brigot, a New Orleans merchant and man of money, and the *entrepreneur de batiments,* as a building contractor was then known, was Joseph Marie Fernandez, who agreed, on January 31, 1834, to do the job for $22,800 and complete it by September 15, or forfeit $25 a day. The original contract has attached to it the pen-and-ink sketch for the design of the ironwork on the long balcony of the second floor which runs the front of Royal and the length of Toulouse Street. Each floor window on the Royal Street facade, it will be observed, has its individual tiny balcony.

On the ground floor of 605 Royal was located in 1838 the bookshop of Leon J. Fremaux, who published in 1876 an odd book with quaint illustrations which he called *New Orleans Characters,* a work now much in demand by collectors. In the upper floors was the studio of Jacques G. L. Amans, a popular portrait painter and native of Belgium, who came to New Orleans in 1830. The pigments from his palette, brushed on by a skillful hand, transformed many a piece of blank canvas into the likenesses of belles and beaux of the *ancien régime.* Today Amans' portraits, usually to be found in peeling gold frames, are prized by those who seek these century-old likenesses of the Creole aristocrats of old New Orleans, and many are on exhibition in the Cabildo.

In the apartments at 607 Royal Street, Denis Prieur lived with his brother Alexandre. Denis Prieur was mayor of New Orleans for six terms, from 1828 to 1838, and again in 1842 when, after election, he resigned to become recorder of mortgages. He holds the record for having been elected mayor more times than any of his predecessors or those who followed him into office.

GOVERNOR ROMAN'S RESIDENCE   611 ROYAL ST.

We are now in a block of Royal Street where every building lining both sides of the narrow thoroughfare is either of ancient or historic importance, for above the shops the crème de la crème of Creole society was housed more than a hundred years ago. Our attention will probably zigzag across the street a great deal as we minutely inspect each structure pointed out.

This solidly built brick building is a twin structure to the more famous one next door. In its upper apartments lived André Bienvenu Roman, twice governor of Louisiana and prominent sugar planter from the *paroisse Saint-Jacques.* When in New Orleans his upstairs apartments were frequently the scenes of brilliant social soirees, and he delighted in giving sumptuous banquets to notables visiting the city. It was Governor Roman who had the State of Louisiana officially subscribe to John James Audubon's mammoth volumes, *The Birds of America.* So when the bird artist revisited the Crescent City in 1837, planter Roman was host to Audubon at dinner served in these upstairs apartments, which was attended by the foremost folk of New Orleans. Such a rich meal was in marked contrast to the reception Audubon received during the dreary days of 1821 when he trod the narrow *banquettes* of the narrow streets a penniless, heartsick, and hungry individual endeavoring to earn a meager living by making pencil sketches of such citizens who would part with a dollar or two for a striking likeness . . . and inwardly wishing his subject was a bird.

The two places where the noted bird artist had his living quarters and studios when in New Orleans in 1821-22 still exist. His first studio in Barracks Street near Royal is now numbered 706 Barracks Street, and the "Little House in Dauphine Street" is now numbered 505 Dauphine.

"COURT OF THE TWO SISTERS"   613 ROYAL ST.

Made famous by the many pictorial reproductions made of its deep and handsome courtyard, this three-story brick building, called in late years the "Court of the Two Sisters," has departed from its former exclusive status of a private residence and is now a restaurant.

Built in 1832, as was its adjoining twin, by Zénon Cavalier while he was president of the *Banque d'Orléans,* it was alloted a much larger court space than the one next door. The site had been owned for many years by Antoine Cavalier, one of the early settlers of the city, who gave it to his son.

The spacious and often photographed courtyard at one time had in the rear left-hand corner a fountain, from which a little fat bronze cupid blew water out of a twisted ram's horn. A few years ago, sad to relate, a purchaser who balked in his intention to convert the house and its courtyard into a jazz palace, "retaliated" by uprooting the fountain and selling it. The little copper Eros is now installed in another delightful patio at 731 Royal Street.

The courtyard gained its popular name from the fact that two sisters, Emma and Bertha Camors, for twenty years, 1886 to 1906, here conducted a fancy and variety store. Sister Emma was Mrs. Raphael Musso. Sister Bertha married Victor Baldomero Angaud, son of Emile Angaud, the boot and shoe merchant, who owned the "Court of the Two Sisters."

DOCTOR DEVEZE'S RESIDENCE   612 ROYAL ST.

Let us desert the left-hand side of the street and inspect the house next to the old Ducatel dry goods emporium. Ownership of the site can be traced back as far as 1794 when Jean Baptiste Lille Sarpy purchased the land and the inconspicuous buildings then on it.

"SPANISH COURTYARD"   616 ROYAL ST.

Adjoining the old Devéze residence is a structure with a most interesting patio,

The Wishing Gates, at 616 Royal St. (etching by M. B. Kendall)

known at one time as "The Spanish Arms Courtyard." It is a twin to the one adjoining it on the lower side, for both were built by Dr. Isadore Labatut in 1831 during the heyday of stylish social migration to this part of the Vieux Carré.

At the end of the tunnel-like corridor, barring the way to the court, are the so-called "Wishing Gates" greatly admired and photographed by visitors. However, these gates were not originally a part of this old mansion but were placed in the corridor in 1931, being removed from the entrance of the old Masonic Temple when that edifice was demolished to make way for the present skyscraper. This would fix the age of the iron gates at about a hundred years, for the old Masonic Temple was built in 1891. Why they should be called the Wishing Gates is not clear—unless the wish is father to the thought.

GRAIHLE'S HOME   621 ROYAL ST.

On the left-hand side of Royal Street is an ancient twin three-story brick building, each side having, as have all other prominent structures in the Old Quarter, a typical courtyard. In 1838 here lived Alexandre Graihle, a noted New Orleans lawyer. As his wife was also prominent their home was the scene of many brilliant social events when this part of *rue Royale* was the Park Avenue of the elect.

Courtyard at 621 Royal St. (drawn by G. F. Castelden)

THE LABATUT MANSION   623 ROYAL ST.

Next to the mansion just described and separated from its twin by a narrow party wall is the old home of a distinguished Orleanian, Jean Baptiste Labatut, a French merchant who came to Louisiana in 1781 to set up in business. Four years after his arrival he married Marie Félicite Saint-Martin, daughter of a distinguished Louisiana family and whose father once owned the section across the Mississippi River directly opposite the Vieux Carré which we today name Algiers. Soon after his marriage the young Frenchman erected his home on this site, although it was then only a modest structure with an *entresol.*

J. B. Labatut was at one time attorney general of the *Illustrious Cabildo,* the city's ruling commission, and was treasurer of New Orleans when Louisiana was transferred by Spain to France. When the British under Pakenham invaded Louisiana, General Labatut was made an aide by Andrew Jackson and placed in charge of the defenses of the city. The original Labatut home was the center of many activities in the closing days of Spanish rule and in the early days of the American domination. In the spring of 1821 General Labatut had his old home enlarged and rebuilt to its present proportions, dividing the spacious courtyard and the house into separate establishments.

DOCTOR LABATUT'S HOME   624 ROYAL ST.

Directly across the street from General Labatut's old home is the residence erected by his son, Dr. Isadore Labatut, in 1831 to house his young bride, Caroline Urquhart, daughter of Thomas Urquhart, a prominent merchant of the old city. On the massive cypress doors that guard the domed corridor leading to a rear court and a stairway ascending to the floors above can be seen the physician's nameplate.

For many years, the descendants of Dr. Labatut, the distinguished Puig family, occupied the old home. For it was Magin Puig y Ferrer, of Catalona, Spain, who won the hand and heart of Caroline Labatut, the physician's eldest daughter. In this splendid old home were spacious rooms with high ceilings filled with fine old furniture, while priceless oil portraits of distinguished Louisianians hung on the walls.

On Monday, December 8, 1794, this property was owned by François Mayronne. While devout Catholics were observing the Feast of the Immaculate Conception, some children playing in the courtyard started a fire in the stables. In less than an hour this section of the city was in flames and when, after hours of fire fighting, the flames died down El Baron de Carondelet, the Spanish governor, took stock and found the entire business section of the city had been wiped out—212 buildings consumed. Only two escaped the fury of the flames, the Cavalier *casa* opposite the scene of the start of the fire, and the commercial house of Don Juan Francisco Merieult in Royal Street.

"ROYAL CASTILIAN ARMS"   628 ROYAL ST.

Even during the days when Spanish masters governed Louisiana the building immediately adjoining Dr. Labatut's was an old structure. In such a domicile the owner combined his business activities on the street floor with all the comforts of home in the living apartments above. There, away from the hurly burly of commercial activities (if there was hurly burly in those leisurely mañana days of the Dons), the family of the merchant kept clear of the trials of trade, for mothers and daughters never mixed their social life with father's trading tribulations. Doubtless many a business transaction was made difficult by the sound of laughter from the rooms above the store, or, possibly, a late afternoon's gossiping bee between a half-dozen who knew all that was going on in the old town proved interesting to those listening in at the store below. The French had a very expressive name for such a tongue-clacking conference . . . they were then, and are now, for that matter, called a *"gumbo ya-ya!"*

Patio at 628 Royal St. (drawn by Clarence Millet)

This building was, in the 1930s and 1940s, a small hotel known as the "Royal Castilian Arms." The house was doubtless erected soon after the second fire, probably during the year 1795, by Charles Loubies, a wealthy Saint Charles Parish planter.

"PATTI'S COURT" 627 ROYAL ST.

This two-story, square-looking building, probably the oldest save one now standing in Royal Street, was at one time the home and mercantile establishment of Antoine Cavalier, who had married Françoise Carrière, and was related, according to tradition, to the same family from which sprung Robert Cavalier, Sieur de la Salle, the knightly adventurer and prince of explorers who after paddling down the length of the Mississippi named the wilderness for Louis XIV, King of France.

As far back as 1777, so the tattered pages of the acts of Jean Baptiste Garic, the scrivener who served as notary under five French and three Spanish governors, tell us, Antoine Cavalier here set up his establishment. Whether or not this is the same house is only conjectural for we must not forget that two disastrous fires, one in 1788 and the other in 1794, swept the center of the town clear of buildings. However, we learn from the dispatches of El Baron de Carondelet that only two of the houses in the main part of the city escaped the fire of December 8, 1794—this, the Cavalier *casa*, and the home and business place of Jean François Merieult, which has already been described.

Today, the old Cavalier home, with its sprawling, interesting patio, is known as "Patti's Court." Local tradition has it that a golden-voiced songbird, Adelina Patti, lived in this home while her voice was making history at the French Opera House and setting musical New Orleans in a furor.

"La petite Patti" paid her second visit to the Crescent City late in 1860 to fulfill a concert engagement. Her director was Maurice Strakosch, who had married her sister Amalia, and the three arrived in the city just as music lovers were planning to patronize the newly constructed opera house which had been opened by an Italian operatic troupe in November. As the troupe's prima donnas had not lived up to the exacting expectations of the music-loving community, the new palace of music was about to register a dismal failure. It was at this critical juncture that the seventeen-year-old Patti was induced to cancel her proposed concerts and appear in the opera house and thus "save the season."

Her New Orleans debut was made on December 19, 1860, in the title role of *Lucia d'Lammermoor* with her brother-in-law, Maestro Strakosch, conducting the orchestra, and the result was an instantaneous hit. Role after role followed and in each the youthful star with the marvelous soprano created a sensation. In no time at all New Orleans was at her feet. The night after Christmas, appearing as Lady Henriette in *Martha,* her rendition of "The Last Rose of Summer" endeared her to all who listened to the liquid notes that filled the vast auditorium. Swiftly followed *Il Barbiere di Siviglia;* Leonore, in *Il Trovatore;* Gilda, in *Rigoletto;* Valentine, in *Les Huguenots;* and there were jammed houses at every performance when Adelina Patti was advertised to appear.

Therefore, one need not be surprised to learn that the *pension* of the darling of the city became a center of attraction, and the beaux, young and old, paraded *rue Royale* praying for, at least, a glimpse of the beautiful young star.

The Old Town Praline & Gift Shop, which occupies one of the ground-floor stores, can be used to pass into and inspect the unique and memory-drenched courtyard.

THE LEMONNIER MANSION   640 ROYAL ST.

Our sight-seeing walk down old *rue Royale* has brought us to what many who know the old Quarter best consider the most interesting building in the Vieux Carré— the bulky four-story brick structure on the southeast corner of Royal and St. Peter streets, usually pointed out as New Orleans' "first skyscraper" and, if you are willing to be misled by an iron plaque on its Royal Street wall, it was built in 1774. It has three names . . . "Doctor LeMonnier's Home," "The Sky-scraper Building," and "Sieur George's House."

George W. Cable, whose stories of old New Orleans gave him an unquestioned rank among the foremost American novelists, was responsible for the third name, for it was in this very building that he domiciled his celebrated fictional character "Sieur George." Today the structure is as Cable described it in the nineteenth century . . . "with its gray stucco peeling off in broad patches, it has a solemn look of gentility in rags, and stands, or, as it were, hangs, about the corner of two ancient streets like a faded fop who pretends to be looking for employment."

According to a popular tale that has been told and retold for many years, this was the first structure in the old town to be erected more than two stories high. It was freely predicted then that the soft oozy soil could not support a building of such unprecedented height and consequently there was danger that this four-story building would tip over and crush its innocent neighbors!

That's the fabulous tradition—here are the facts. Pedro Pedesclaux, one of the best known of the notaries in New Orleans under the Spanish and American domination, owned this site and lived here in a house with one story. In 1806 he planned a new edifice on this corner and to finance the project set about raising the needed money by subscription.

But by 1811 *Maison Pedesclaux* had not been built so the site was offered for sale by those who had put up the money. Dr. Yves LeMonnier, a well-known practising physician, and François Grandchamps, the druggist whose pharmacy we have already seen at the corner of Royal and St. Louis streets, were the purchasers for $16,000. The new owners immediately engaged the services of two engineers and architects whose names are familiar to those who know the story of the Battle of New Orleans . . . Arsène Lacarrière Latour, General Jackson's principal engineer, and Hyacinthe Laclotte, the engineer whose engraving of that famous battle has been frequently reproduced. Latour and Laclotte set to work immediately; the walls of the *entresol* were heightened and the third story and roof added. Five months after they made their bargain with Dr. LeMonnier, the *maison* was completed and ready for occupancy—the $7,600 promised the architects for their work was paid on November 13, 1811.

SIEUR
GEORGES
HOUSE

©M.H.HOBBS   OLD NEW ORLEANS

*Built in 1811 this aged house at Royal and St. Peter streets is known as Dr. LeMonnier's
Home, "The Sky-scraper Building," and "'Sieur George's House."
One of the most interesting structures in the Old Square.*

Dr. LeMonnier moved into the two upper stories, the ground-floor shops were rented to merchants, and the physician selected for his study the beautiful corner oval room on the third floor—declared by some architects as the finest room in New Orleans. From its corner window one can look out upon, as the good *docteur* many times doubtless did, the iron-girded balcony which still bears his exquisitely wrought *Y L M* monogram. The balcony railings on the LeMonnier mansion are worthy of minute attention—three of them are edged by fine wrought-iron work and in the center of each is the physician's initials.

Ten years after moving into this splendid new structure, Dr. LeMonnier became its sole owner. François Grandchamps, in financial difficulties, was forced by creditors to sell his interest in the building. After Dr. LeMonnier's death in 1832, the property passed to his four children, and the two upper stories as well as the ground floors were rented out. The occupant of the corner shop in 1849 was a grocer named Jean Fisse, but by 1860 he had saved enough to purchase the building from Dr. LeMonnier's daughter, Marie Jeanne, then the wife of Paul M. Petit who lived in Paris.

Grocer Fisse remained the building's owner until 1876, when a court order forced him to sell to Bertrand Saloy. It was Saloy, who began his business career as an old clothes and bottle man on the Old Basin, who, *after* December 11, 1876, *added the fourth story* to the old LeMonnier mansion.

As originally built by Major Latour, the "skyscraper" had four shops in the *rez-de-chaussée,* or ground floor; there were six rooms on the second, and seven rooms on the top or third story. A garden was laid out on the terraced roof, and the courtyard was paved with Barsac stones.

After Bertrand Saloy purchased the LeMonnier mansion in 1876 and added the fourth story, he turned this distinctive edifice into a tenement and here, if you prefer Cable's fiction (and most folk do), came Monsieur George—the common folk of the neighborhood shortening the respectful address to 'Sieur—with his mysterious little hair-trunk which he guarded so carefully, so mysteriously. When slyly opened by the landlord "Kookoo," the trunk was found stuffed full of, not greenbacks, but lottery tickets long outdated which had failed to bring fortune to the pathetic 'Sieur George. That is why the LeMonnier mansion, built in 1811 only three stories high, is frequently pointed out as " 'Sieur George's House."

Wrought-iron balcony with monogram of Dr. Yves LeMonnier

"GREEN SHUTTER SHOP"   710 St. Peter St.

Few buildings in the Old Square, great or small, can boast an antiquity which exceeds that possessed by a quaint one-story structure with green shutters at 710 St. Peter Street. Records written nearly two centuries ago prove that this *maison basse en briques*, as it was then described, was standing in the years when the Spanish ruled their *Nueva Orléans*.

This house with the green shutters was built before 1796 by Don Lorenzo Gachet, and here he lived until he passed on and the unobtrusive structure went to his widow. Taking its popular name from the color of its shutters, the old Gachet home is now one of the many quaint and unique shops in the Quarter.

LACOUL RESIDENCE   714 St. Peter St.

Many consider this building one of the representative old homes of the Vieux Carré—its small quaint court and fine stairway leading from the corridor to the second story have long attracted artists. While it was built May 19, 1829, by Dr. Yves LeMonnier, it is best known as the town house of George Raymond Lacoul, who became owner when Dr. LeMonnier's children sold it in 1838.

In 1860 the tenant was Antoine Alciatore, who turned the place into a boardinghouse, serving here the cookery that afterwards brought him culinary fame. After he left the Lacoul house, Antoine purchased and opened his well-known St. Louis Street restaurant in 1862.

CASA DE FLECHIER   718 St. Peter St.

This interesting old mansion with its plastered facade and pilasters extending from foundation to roof, betraying an Egyptian influence in their design, has for many years erroneously been pointed out as the home of the ancient *Le Théâtre de la rue Saint-Pierre*, the first playhouse to be erected in old New Orleans. That celebrated theatre was two houses away, so we will find.

This ancient residence was the town house of a prominent planter, Etienne Marie de Fléchier, who apparently erected his *casa grande* soon after acquiring the site in 1792. In 1817 the Widow Fléchier, she who had been Françoise Dussan de la Croix, sold the residence to John Garnier, planter, commission merchant, and brick maker, whose kilns were located at the head of Poydras Street and the river. The road to the Garnier brickyards followed what is now Carondelet Street and that old roadway was known, in consequence, as *rue de la briqueterie*. This was before the street was named for Governor the Baron de Carondelet and the adjoining *calle* christened with the title of his wife—Baronne.

Fléchier's old *casa* is today the famous Pat O'Brien's bar. Its courtyard is one of the finest in the Vieux Carré.

FAISENDIEU'S *POSADA*   726 St. Peter St.

Probably no other courtyard in the Vieux Carré has been more admired and pictured than the patio of the old Faisendieu *posada* or tavern. This particular court has long been one of the showplaces of the Quarter and the wrought-iron gates, although of recent construction, are most interesting.

Like the mansions on either side, this old inn has had many owners. Our search of documents scribbled in Spanish by *escribanos* not distinguished for their handling of a crow quill shows that on June 18, 1803, Don Antonio Faisendieu gave Don Geronimo Gros 7,200 *pesos* for the property, which was then described as lying between the home of Don Esteban Fléchier and *El Coliseo*, the St. Peter Street theatre. This would indicate Señor Gros built the place and not Don Antonio. Be that as it may, we can be sure of one thing . . . that it was standing and inhabited when the banner of Castile and Leon waved over the old city. An early directory informs us that Antonio Faisendieu was a tavern keeper at 23 *Saint-Pierre* in the early days of the American occupation, and in 1809 a notarial act states that the old inn was *"située en cette ville rue St. Pierre avec une maison à étage construite en brique . . . joignant d'un côté au terrain de Monsieur Marie De Flétcher et de l'autre au Spectacle,"* thus again definitely fixing the location of the St. Peter Street theatre. The old *posada* is now the home of Preservation Hall, one of the few places left in the city where one can go to hear classic New Orleans jazz performed.

LE SPECTACLE   732 ST. PETER ST.

For many years the actual site of the famed first theatre in New Orleans has been the subject of conjecture and, unfortunately, the building at 716 St. Peter Street was usually pointed out to visitors as the ancient home of theatrics and opera. Fortunately notarial records exist that fix the exact location of the old *Spectacle*, if not the building itself. Does the house at 732 St. Peter Street rest on the foundations of the old theatre or has every vestige of that historic edifice disappeared? *¿Quien sabe?* That is something the yellowed pages of the acts of such notaries as Jean Garic, Narcisse Broutin, Michel de Armas, Esteban de Quinones, Carlos Ximenes, Pedro Pedesclaux, and Andres Almonester y Roxas fail to disclose.

What we have gleaned from these old documents proves that on July 27, 1790, Louis Chevalier de Macarty purchased at *"Comprado en publica almoneda,"* or public auction, this property from Juan Doreto del Postigo, *auditor de guerre y assessor gral.* A year later, June 4, 1791, in two sales, Don Luis Alessandro Henrique secured two pieces of property, one from Chevalier Macarty and the other from Geronimo, both being described as lying between the lands of Pedro Lambert (who owned the Bourbon Street corner site) and François Collell, who in 1792 sold his property to Don Esteban de Fléchier.

In 1791 a troupe of strolling actor folk landed in New Orleans from Cape François, Santo Domingo. They were headed by Louis Blaize Tabary and had been driven out of the West Indies island by an uprising of the blacks. It was then the title *"El Coliseo"* (Spanish for playhouse) was given the house. Performances began at this time and continued under Bernardo Coquer until the place was closed by the authorities . . . why this was necessary is not recorded, possibly because its *rez-de-chaussée* became a notorious ballroom.

From 1793 the playhouse went by the name of *La Salle de Comédie* in letters written by citizens who preferred to write, and speak, their native French tongue. The

Santo Domingo troupe, having neither hall nor place for their performances, were content with appearing in parlors of private houses and in halls they could rent. Often the artists had to present their dramatic sketches under improvised tents, we are told. As most of the artists were refugees from France and incarnate demagogues, it is said they frequently interpolated between the lines of their parts some of the songs of *La Terreur* of the French revolutionists, such as *La Carmagnole*, the *Cà-Ira*, all calculated to rouse the ire of the royalists. Disorder ensued and became so frequent that the police were forced to close the showhouse.

Performances continued off and on for a number of years after New Orleans became an American city. In 1821 *Théâtre Saint-Pierre* was sold by General J. B. Labatut and it appears the new owners erected the present building on the foundations of the colorful old playhouse.

THE HEART OF THE VIEUX CARRE

On our return to Royal Street we will arrive again at what has well been termed the heart of the Vieux Carré, and here it is that you may or may not want to continue the Royal Street promenade to the lower end of the Old Square so that a return sight-seeing trip may be made up Chartres Street. That being the case, you can follow St. Peter Street in the direction of the river to inspect the Saint Louis Cathedral, Cabildo, Presbytère, and the Pontalba buildings fronting the old *Place d'Armes*, which we now call Jackson Square.

Whether you elect to continue down the length of *rue Royale* or not, there are several interesting buildings to inspect, and shops to visit, in St. Peter Street, on the river side of Royal. So let us look them over, especially *Le Petit Salon*, a gathering place of New Orleans' distinguished women, and the famous "Little Theatre."

MERCIER MANSION   630 ST. PETER ST.

The outside appearance and construction of this two-story plastered-brick building not only identifies it but indicates its antiquity. An inspection of its interior, the

Old fireplace in the kitchen at 630 St. Peter St. (drawn by Leda Plauché)

courtyard, and the old kitchen with its unique fireplace will further fix the impression that this is a very old home. A notarial record of February 3, 1796, proves it to have been owned by Don Juan Bautista Mercier.

LE PETIT SALON   620 St. Peter St.

A group of New Orleans women, animated by a praiseworthy desire to preserve the traditions, culture, and atmosphere of the Vieux Carré, in 1925 purchased one of the distinctive old mansions of the Quarter for their gathering place. In such fashion did the old David mansion become *Le Petit Salon*, one of the foremost and most exclusive organizations of its kind in the country. Mrs. Elizabeth Meriwether Gilmer, best known to the world as *Times-Picayune* columnist "Dorothy Dix," was once the president of the Little Salon.

This residence was built in 1838 by Victor David, a wealthy merchant, and replaced another old home which had its foundations laid by Don Juan Bautista Orso when New Orleans was a Spanish possession, who purchased the site from the distinguished Trudeau family. From the time of its completion until 1867 it was the residence of the David family and a number of others called the place home before it was purchased and restored to its former grandeur by the ladies of New Orleans.

The mansion has long attracted attention, being distinctive for the ironwork that lines its three balconies, as well as for the solid iron bars that guard the ground floor, and the railing on its curving outside steps leading to the second-floor balcony. It will be seen that each balcony railing is of a different design. Notice the celebrated "bow and arrow" motif—although the arrows are of orthodox shape the bow that binds them where they cross is not the kind of bow used to propel arrows but the sort of bow you form with a ribbon! Does this mean that two of the arrows used by Archer Dan Cupid are tied together for all time by a lover's knot? Whatever the meaning, this is a unique conceit, one to be found only in a city where balcony ironwork has tested the skill and ingenuity of skilled ironworkers.

The bow and arrow balcony railing of Le Petit Salon

O'HARA'S SNUFF FACTORY   622 ST. PETER ST.

Adjoining the old Mercier mansion, a century and more ago, was the residence and business place of Demoiselle Nancy O'Hara, for on the ground floor was Mlle O'Hara's "snuff and segar manufactury." Nancy O'Hara purchased the property in 1817 from Dame Marianne Rivarde, widow of Jean Ostin, and it is quite probable that the foundations of the present building date from that time. The third story, however, has been added since and the facade refaced with modern brick in the past century.

THE ARSENAL   615 ST. PETER ST.

The building opposite *Le Petit Salon* and in the immediate rear of the Cabildo was, from 1840 until 1915, the state arsenal. During the celebration of the centennial of the Battle of New Orleans the old structure was turned over to the Louisiana State Museum to become the state's "Battle Abbey" in which exhibits commemorating the valor of Louisianians at war could be housed. Here were seen relics of the early Indian wars; of the Revolutionary period, when Galvez's expedition against the British in West Florida gave Louisiana a part in that historic era; of the War of 1812, especially the battle of New Orleans; the Civil War; the Spanish-American War; and World War I.

The Arsenal, which occupied the site of the old prison of the Spanish, was erected from designs drawn by James Harrison Dakin and cost $19,500. When the building agreement was signed by Governor A. B. Roman on July 1, 1839, the contractor agreed to construct it in five months. On January 1, 1840, the new arsenal was finished and occupied by the Louisiana Legion, whose monogram *L L* below a pair of crossed cannon and a pile of cannonballs is still to be seen on the iron balcony facing Orleans Alley. The Louisiana Legion was an aristocratic military organization whose officers and men were drawn from the best Creole and American families. It was from this armory that the members of the Orleans Artillery set

Monogram and crossed cannons, insignia of the Louisiana Legion

Orleans or Pirates' Alley (drawn by Clarence Millet)

off for their activities in the war with Mexico. During the Civil War both the Confederate and Union forces made use of it. The building has remained a part of the Louisiana State Museum complex.

Adjoining the Arsenal are two buildings, which also occupy a portion of the site upon which once stood the ancient *Calabozo* . . . the "calaboose," as many of us prefer to pronounce the word. Both were purchased by William Ratcliffe Irby and presented to the Louisiana State Museum. Both side on Arsenal Alley, which was officially named *Passage de la Bourse* in 1840 when the city made a portion of the old prison ground a short walkway from St. Peter to Orleans Passage. The residence fronting St. Peter Street, now reconstructed and bearing the number 619, was built in 1842 by Hugh Montgomery Dowlin, a house and sign painter. For a number of years it served as a meeting place for the Colonial Dames and the U.S. Daughters of 1812, who named it "Jackson House," thus honoring the general who saved New Orleans from invasion, although, of course, "Old Hickory" never occupied it. The other old residence, which faces the side wall of the Saint Louis Cathedral, and Orleans Passage, was also erected in 1842 by Hugh Dowlin. It too is now used for museum purposes.

LITTLE THEATRE   616 ST. PETER ST.

The Little Theatre of New Orleans or, to give it its dignified official name, *Le Petit Théâtre du Vieux Carré,* was founded to foster the presentation of worthwhile dramatic art and to keep alive not only histrionic art but the traditions of the Old Square. In 1916 an organization, known then as the Drawing Room Players, gave dramatic productions in the drawing rooms of the homes of the members. In 1919 they had their own rented "theatre" on the second floor of one of the St. Ann Street Pontalba buildings. So great was the artistic and financial success achieved by these talented amateurs that they erected their own playhouse in 1922, selecting

Le Petit Théâtre du Vieux Carré reflects the architecture of old New Orleans in a splendid restoration (drawn and copyrighted by Morris Henry Hobbs)

a site in the very heart of the Vieux Carré and constructing a building that reflected the architecture of the Quarter, being modeled after the facade of the Old Absinthe House. The patio of *Le Petit Théâtre du Vieux Carré* is a beautiful piece of restoration and should be seen by the visitor.

LABRANCHE BUILDINGS   700 ROYAL ST.

Among the characteristic sights of the Vieux Carré that the visitor to New Orleans remembers long after his return home are the delicate traceries in wrought and cast iron which embroider so many balconies on the ancient buildings which huddle closely together in the narrow streets of the old city. Probably no other structure holds a greater attraction to a visitor strolling down Royal Street than the building at the northeast corner of that street where it meets St. Peter. Because of its prominent grille of cast iron, it has been popularly called the "lacework building." The design, of entwined oak leaves and acorns, is acknowledged as one of the fine examples of cast iron found in a city noted for such balcony decoration.

This particular structure, so handsomely decorated, stands like a brawny sentinel guarding the other buildings in the small square bounded by Royal, St. Peter, Orleans Passage, and old Arsenal Alley. All of these buildings, save one, were built between 1835 and 1840 by Jean Baptiste Labranche, a prominent and wealthy sugar planter of Saint Charles Parish, and his widow.

Along this block are a number of shops which specialize in the celebrated candy of old New Orleans—the *praline*. The *praline* is a concoction of sugar and pecan nuts, a confection as old as the town itself. It is a crisp candy made from nut-kernels boiled in sugar. In France the praline was made by cooking almonds in sugar, called *amande rissolée dans du sucre*. When the early colonists came to Louisiana the housewife substituted the native pecans for the almonds in making the candy. The name *praline* is derived from that of a French marshal and diplomat, César du Plessis-Praslin, later the duc de Choiseul. It was Marshal Praslin who, according to tradition, first ordered his almonds cooked in sugar and, as his name Praslin is pronounced "pra-lin," that designation became fastened upon the favorite and distinctive candy made by the early French inhabitants of Louisiana.

It was during the golden boom days of the late 1830s that Jean Baptiste Labranche purchased the land composing this square, except one plot, and erected the buildings now standing there. Planter Labranche, who had made his fortune growing sugar, decided to invest a part of it in the very heart of the old city. The name he bore is a noted one in Louisiana. His paternal ancestor who came to the colony in 1724 from Metz, Germany, was Johan Zweig. In 1737, when settler Zweig's son Johan married Suzanne Marchand, a young French orphan reared by the Ursuline nuns, the French notary called upon to draw up the marriage contract had difficulty in spelling the name of the bridegroom—so he translated it. Being told that *zweig* meant "twig" in German, and twig translated into French meant "branch," notary Henri, unable to tussle successfully with the orthography of a name containing the letter "w," without further ado dubbed the husband-to-be "Jean Labranche." So the name has remained ever since.

The Labranche building, at Royal and St. Peter streets, because of its cast-iron balcony decorations, is the most photographed structure in old New Orleans (drawn and copyrighted by Morris Henry Hobbs)

Therefore, oak leaves and acorns provide a most appropriate motif for the cast iron decorating the balcony railings of the house Jean Baptiste Labranche built.

CADET'S BAKERY   701 ROYAL ST.

On the downtown woods corner of Royal and St. Peter streets, we see the same brick building that once-upon-a-time housed the famous bakery of Cadet Molon. Not only were the round and twisted brown loaves that were shoveled hot and fragrant out of Cadet's ovens considered among the best that could be purchased in old New Orleans, but it was this same master bread baker who many times supplied, gratis, Père Antoine with bread that the celebrated Capuchin priest distributed to the poor and hungry. The rear building on the St. Peter Street side is only a remnant of what was Cadet's old *boulangerie* once notable for a high quaint chimney that rose above the tiled roof of the bakery.

Just how many years this corner building can claim is not known—suffice it to say that Jacques Molon purchased the site from Ignacio Dominique on April 8, 1789, and not long afterwards he probably erected the bakery which passed on to his son Jacques (the name *Cadet* was used to designate the second son in a family) and Cadet Molon carried on here the bakery business until 1824, when he was succeeded by Joseph Vincent, whose confectionery shop was a favorite rendezvous for those with a sweet tooth.

In the days that Cadet and the other bakers of the city supplied their patrons with the staff of life, the size of the loaf purchased was regulated by city ordinance, and the ordinance was regulated by the supply of flour reaching the city on flatboats making the journey down the Ohio and Mississippi rivers. A loaf of bread, weighing thirty-one ounces, cost a bit.

A bit, to those who may be puzzled by the term, is just one half of two bits, and two bits, you know, is a quarter of a dollar or twenty-five cents. The bit is an old New Orleans institution, transferred to the West during the days of old and the days of gold and the days of '49. Even before the Crescent City became an American town, the Mexican trade dollar was the unit of trade. Small change was difficult to obtain, such as the *sueldo*, the *dinero*, *maravedi*, and *ochavo*. True there were such small Spanish coins as the *picayune* and the *cuartillo* (this became a quartee to the ignorant) but not enough of them to go around the marts of trade. So, to make change, frequently the big round Mexican silver dollar was physically cut in pieces—or should we say, cut into bits! Slice a trade dollar into two equal halves

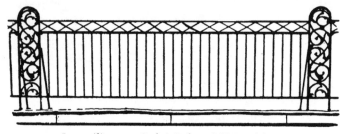

Iron railing over Cadet's Bakery, 701 Royal St.

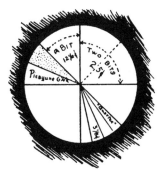

and you have two half-dollars. When each half was again halved, you had two quarters. To make still smaller change you could cut the quarters into two equal parts, and you had two *bits*. A bit was so-called because the two *bits*, when placed point to point, resembled a *bitte* or, as the English-speaking had it, the "bitt-head" on the fore deck of a boat on which hawsers were made fast. At least, that is one explanation of the origin of the term bit.

Other quaint Spanish coin-words, persisting in the Old Square today, are *picayune* and *cuartee* (sometimes spelled "quartee," properly a *cuartillo* and now given a value of 2 1/2 cents). The word *picayune* has found its way into our English dictionaries and means "anything of trifling value." The expression *lagniappe* (pronounced "lan-yap") may also be heard. It is composed of the French *la* and Spanish *napa*, "that which is thrown in gratis." Listen to a little Creole boy sent to the corner grocery with a nickel: "My maman say gimme *cuartee* red beans an' *cuartee* rice . . . with *oignon* for *lagniappe*!"

DR. MARTIN'S MANSION   709 ROYAL ST.

A typical mansion of the old section, erected during the golden boom days, is the structure adjoining Cadet Molon's old bakery. It became the home of Dr. Joseph Auguste Thérez Martin, a socially prominent physician, soon after April 23, 1831, when he contracted with James Loughrea to erect the mansion for $6,918. The house remained Dr. Martin's residence until his death in 1839, when it passed into the possession of his children. Since that time the old place has housed many owners.

ARTS AND CRAFTS CLUB   712 ROYAL ST.

A home of modern art once occupied the old mansion of Dr. Pierre Frédéric Thomas, which the physician had constructed shortly after he purchased the site from Antoine Bienvenu on May 16, 1823. Here Dr. Thomas lived for many years and from the time of his ownership to the present day the old brick edifice has seen many owners and many more tenants. The fact that from its side windows and generous galleries a view could be secured of the green of the Cathedral Garden and of the activities of Royal Street, for that ancient thoroughfare was a busy merchandising street in those good old days, has always made this a valuable structure. It is the only house in this square that was not erected by J. B. Labranche.

In 1933 the New Orleans Arts and Crafts Club, a local organization that had for its object the tutoring of those interested in art, and which for a number of years was domiciled in the old Seignouret mansion, moved to this location and established its galleries and art rooms. Here budding artists found full opportunity to put on canvas the picturesqueness of the Vieux Carré and display the product of their brushes.

CATHEDRAL GARDEN   ROYAL AT ORLEANS

Reaching the corner of Royal and Orleans streets, we should glance across the street and note the fence-girded lawn lying in the rear of the Saint Louis Cathedral officially known as the Cathedral Garden. It is more popularly called "Saint Anthony's Square," so named in honor of a Spanish Capuchin priest who, according to tradition, lived in this open space in a tiny hut. Unfortunately, for the tradition, this garden was not in existence when the good priest was alive, and the hut was at Orleans Street near Dauphine.

The Capuchin was Padre Antonio de Sedella, who first came to Louisiana about 1779. His purpose, so tradition tells us, was to introduce into the then Spanish colony, the Holy Inquisition. He, however, appeared to have kept this a secret from the governor, Don Esteban Miro, for a year or more, but when he made it known, the governor had him expelled from the colony. When this expulsion took place is not definitely known and it is even denied by some that Fray Antonio was a representative of the Inquisition. However, in the records of the *Illustrious Cabildo,* of January 25, 1788, we find that the priest, then evidently in Spain, had sent the members of that body a communication asking for a certificate of good character. In it he was named "commissioner of the Inquisition of Faith."

About 1795 Padre Antonio returned to New Orleans and was installed as pastor of Saint Louis Cathedral, but this time he came to the colony with the intention of gaining converts with holy water and not by holy fire. He became a well-known and well-beloved figure in old New Orleans, although he did quarrel with other members of the clergy.

Whenever Padre Antonio appeared on the streets, with cowled head and sandaled feet, and a bag hanging from his girdle filled with small coins, all the children of the Quarter followed after him, like the children of Hamelin after the Pied Piper. The urchins would kneel down in the muddy streets to ask his blessing and never failed to demand that a *lagniappe,* in the shape of a *picayune* or a "*quartee,*" be thrown in with the blessing—the priest never refused either. And the poor always got the left-over loaves of bread that baker Cadet Molon furnished the Capuchin. The better folk of the city demanded that the padre officiate at the christenings, marriages, and funerals and when Fray Antonio got into a tremendous quarrel with Father Walsh, the town folk sided with the Capuchin and a merry church war ensued.

Francisco Antonio Ildefonso Moreno y Arze was the legitimate son of Pedro Moreno and Anna Arze and was born, November 18, 1748, in Sedella, diocese of

Orleans Street looking towards Royal, the rear of the Cathedral, and the Cathedral Garden. On the left is the old Orleans Ballroom, now a convent for black Catholic nuns. (Drawn by Clarence Millet)

Malaga, Kingdom of Grenada, Spain. That is why he became known as Padre Antonio de Sedella. To the day of his death, January 19, 1829, he was one of the best loved figures of the old city, and was accompanied to his resting place in the Cathedral by an immense procession of citizens, including the entire membership of Free Masons of New Orleans, which gave rise to the whisper that he was a member of that secret fraternal order.

The narrow passageways on either side of the garden and the Cathedral are called by many names. They were not cut through the block, from Chartres to Royal Street, until 1831. Then they were named *ruelle d'Orléans Nord* and *ruelle d'Orléans Sud.* Later the lower *ruelle* (in French a "narrow street") was called *Passage de Saint-Antoine* or Saint Anthony's Alley, although it is sometimes named "Cloister Alley." The upper is Orleans Passage but many delight in naming it "Pirates' Alley," in spite of the fact that Jean Laffite's pirates had long disappeared from the old city when the authorities made it a walkway in 1831.

ORLEANS BALLROOM   717 ORLEANS ST.

Instead of continuing down Royal Street on our quest for ancient landmarks, we can turn into Orleans Street to inspect one or two of the buildings fronting this old thoroughfare, which engineer de Pauger, when he designed the original city, planned to be the *Grand'rue*, and made it seven feet wider than the other streets in the Old Square. The large building on the downtown side of Orleans Street has had a most interesting history. It has been in turn a ballroom for the elite, state house and legislative hall, district court, home for the early Carnival organizations, and a convent for an order of black Catholic nuns.

Most writers link this former palace of Terpsichore with the place where the famous, or infamous, quadroon balls took place. This is an error. The quadroon balls were held elsewhere, principally at the *Salle de Condé*—at what is now Chartres and Madison streets. This particular building was erected in 1819 by John Davis to adjoin his *Théâtre d'Orléans,* which he had built in 1816 on the burned ruins of the first playhouse. For forty years the *Salle d'Orléans* was the scene of divers activities—some brilliant, some drab. In 1826 a grand ball was given for the Marquis de Lafayette. Two years later, when the government house was destroyed by fire, the state legislature held its meeting within these staunch old walls. Many banquets to many notables were spread in the magnificent central room. It was a swank gathering place for the somebodies of New Orleans. Davis' Rooms continued to be popular with the best elements of New Orleans society until 1838, when the Saint Louis Hotel was completed and its magnificent ballroom thrown open . . . then the *ton* of the Creole city flocked to the newer and more attractive place.

In 1866 the old Orleans Street theatre was destroyed by a fire but the Orleans Ballroom was saved from the flames. When it was offered for sale in 1881, Thomy Lafon, a freeman of color of splendid memory here, was instrumental in securing the property for the Congregation of the Sisters of the Holy Family, an order of black Catholic nuns. He also purchased the property on which the old theatre once rose, and on that site built the present building.

RESTAURANT D'ORLEANS   718 ORLEANS ST.

Directly opposite the old *Salle d'Orléans* is a two-story building erected in 1809 by Antoine Angué. During the heyday of the *Théâtre d'Orléans* and when the best folk of town thronged the Orleans Ballroom, this place gained its fame from the quality of meals served by Creole chefs. It was called the *Restaurant d'Orléans* and for many years was in the charge of Camille Adrien Dupuy who, in 1838, sold his lease to Gabriel Julien, who also catered to the discriminating palates of the best people of the city for many years thereafter.

MAYOR ROFFIGNAC'S   721 ROYAL ST.

Upon our return to *rue Royale* to continue our saunter down this interesting street we should pause for a moment to take a hasty survey of the two-story brick building on the downtown woods corner of Orleans. It was erected by one of the early mayors of New Orleans, Joseph Roffignac, who, before he was forced to flee his native France to escape the guillotine, was Count Louis Philippe Joseph de Roffignac. Another young French nobleman, who was also forced to flee the Revolutionists, was Jacques Pitot de Beaujardière. He accompanied Roffignac to Louisiana. In time both became wealthy merchants in the city of their adoption and, stranger still, each became mayor of New Orleans during the early days of the American domination.

718½ ORLEANS STREET - © M.H. HOBBS - OLD NEW ORLEANS

The entranceway to Camille Dupuy's Restaurant d'Orléans of the gay 1830s

MAISON MONTEGUT   731 ROYAL ST.

Just when the ancient Maison Montegut, one of the landmarks of the Old Square, was erected must always remain a mystery for the only evidence we have as to its age is a notarial act before Carlos Ximenes on June 23, 1799, which proves that it was then occupied by Dr. Joseph Montegut. It is of the Creole-Spanish style of architecture that was followed in building the city after the second disastrous fire of 1794. The patio is distinctive and today it provides an appropriate setting for the fountain, with a fat little cupid in its center, which for many years graced the "Court of the Two Sisters."

LANGUILLE BUILDING   800 ROYAL ST.

Directly opposite the site of the ancient Durel furniture shop at 801 Royal Street is a large brick structure noteworthy for its courtyard, entered on the Royal Street side, which traveled artists declare to be reminiscent of courtyards seen in large Italian cities. For many years the old home, which fronts in St. Ann Street, was the residence of a very old and respected Creole family. In 1801, when the Spanish were masters of New Orleans, Don Francisco Balthazar Languille purchased the site from Don Francisco Picard and built the present house, which was then the highest structure to be erected in old New Orleans—its *first* "skyscraper." In 1828 the builder left the place to his two sons, Jean François and Pierre Joseph Languille. It was not until 1883 that the Languille home passed to other owners.

LEFEBRE BUILDINGS   812 ROYAL ST.

This three-story double-brick building on the river side of Royal has shops on the ground floor. A spacious gallery is decorated with a cast-iron grille which has a motif of bunches of grapes and leaves, a popular design as the visitor will notice the more he penetrates the Old Square. This structure has no particular historic interest and is pointed out as an example of construction in 1832, erected by Felix Lefebre, a coal, lumber, and brick merchant, for commercial purposes.

DUREL'S FURNITURE SHOP   801 ROYAL ST.

There still stands, at the corner of Royal and St. Ann streets, a one-story structure with a tin roof—the half-round Spanish tiles that so intrigued Lafcadio Hearn in 1882 have long since disappeared—a building that has become absolutely shapeless with age. It still deserves that gifted writer's description . . . "a mere hollow carcass, a shattered brick skeleton to which plaster and laths cling in patches only, like shrunken hide upon the bones of some creature left to die and mummify under the sun."

It was Lafcadio Hearn who claimed this decaying structure was the *Café des Réfugiés* but we now know that that coffeehouse, frequented in the very old days by fugitives from the islands of the Antilles, was really situated at 514 St. Philip Street and was run by Jean Baptiste Therot. Later, in 1833, he moved his thirst-quenching business to another location at 287 Old Levee (now 921 Decatur Street), opposite the old French Market and next to the ancient *Hôtel de la Marine.*

There is no question, however, that this corner building has had a varied and interesting career, even if it was never a grog shop frequented by exiles. It was erected in September 1788 by Juan Bautista Durel, to give this Frenchman his Spanish name, who established here what the notarial act called a store of *Linge de Ménage et Meubles*—"Household Linens and Furniture." It remained a dry goods shop and was never a wet goods emporium.

DANIEL CLARK'S HOME   823 ROYAL ST.

A typical old home in the central section of the Vieux Carré is that one once occupied by Alberta Kinsey, noted for her fine oil portraits of courtyards in the old Quarter. In the rear of what was once her studio is one of the typical patios she so deftly portrayed on canvas, and in it grows one of the largest oleanders blooming in downtown New Orleans.

Whether this fine old home was standing when Daniel Clark purchased the property from Gilbert Andry on November 11, 1803, just nine days before New Orleans became an American city, is not now clear, but for years it was Clark's home. Clark was an Irish adventurer picturesquely involved in Louisiana politics, aside from being a leading merchant during the Spanish domination. He served the state as its first representative in the national Congress, was involved in the Burr-Wilkinson imbroglio, and holds the dubious distinction of having shot Governor Claiborne in the leg when that harassed chief executive was bedeviled into calling Clark onto the field of honor.

It was here, in the old Daniel Clark home, that Andrew Jackson was welcomed to the city by Governor Claiborne, Mayor Nicolas Girod, and a large assemblage of officials and citizens, on December 2, 1814, when the famous fighting man arrived

Ancient cuisine of Daniel Clark's, 823 Royal St.

Iron balcony railing at 824 Royal St.

from his Pensacola exploit to save New Orleans from the British invading force under General Pakenham.

821 ROYAL ST.—Adjoining the old Daniel Clark house, this old mansion with a typical arched corridor leading through the *rez-de-chaussée* to a flagged courtyard, was built by Jacques César Paillette in 1811.

825-831-833 ROYAL ST.—On the downtown side of Clark's old home is an interesting old place that was once owned by Juan Tourneboule, according to the Spanish notaries. As a matter of fact he was John Turnbull of the Feliciana district in West Florida, a well-to-do English planter, who purchased the site from Jacques Fletcher in 1790. While the front is not one of the ancients of the street, the court and old rear buildings evidently are very old.

MARCHAND MANSION   830 ROYAL ST.

Opposite the old Daniel Clark home is an interesting building which was erected in 1808 by Salomon Prevost, one of the early lawyers of New Orleans in the American domination who was previously attorney general of the *Illustrious Cabildo*. Today this old home is best known as the Marchand mansion and has proved interesting to architects because of its construction, known to the French as *édifice en colombage,* and for the interesting example of an early winding stairway leading from the rear court to the apartments above.

824 ROYAL ST.—At the time Salomon Prevost was building, Jean Baptiste Dejean had already erected this commodious residence and it, too, is one of the architectural relics of the old street worth at least a passing glance from the visitor. The central panel of the balcony ironwork is of an interesting design.

MADAME POREE'S   840-842 ROYAL ST.

At the corner of Royal and Dumaine streets, on the southeast corner, is a two-story plastered-brick building that at one time was one of the better residences of the old town and was occupied for many years by Thomas Porée and his wife, who was Louise Marguerite Foucher. As becoming the home of those belonging to two of the first families of the city, the Porée mansion was frequently the scene of brilliant social affairs.

Just when the Porée residence was built eludes notarial files. The first transaction on record shows that on March 4, 1808, Thomas Porée purchased the
corner site and *"une belle maison"* from Louis d'Aquin, and it was then described as
being between the properties of Manuel de Lanzos and another piece of ground
owned by d'Aquin, the sale price being $8,430. On June 18, 1818, Mme Porée sold
the mansion for $15,000 to John Martin, thus making it evident that the Porées
made extensive additions to the residence.

"MADAME JOHN'S LEGACY"   632 DUMAINE ST.

Let us interrupt our stroll down Royal Street and turn to the right so we may inspect what is probably the oldest structure now standing in the Vieux Carré and
one that holds a peculiar interest, for it is one of the three houses George W. Cable
described in his short story " 'Tite Poulette," to be found in his book *Old Creole
Days*.

Lafcadio Hearn found it "a very peculiar house" when he was ferreting out the
places in which Cable domiciled his visionary folk . . . "half-brick, half timber that
creates the impression that its builder began it with the intention of erecting a
three-story brick but changed his mind before the first story had been completed
and finished the edifice with second-hand lumber supporting the gallery with
wooden posts that resembled monstrous balusters."

But let Cable tell us how it gained its name. "This was once the home of a gay
young gentleman whose first name happened to be John. He was a member of the
Good Children's Social Club. As his parents lived with him, his wife would, according to custom, have been called Madame John—but he had no wife. His father
died, then his mother, last of all, himself." When dying he told the handsome
quadroon Zalli, who carried in her arms an infant, 'Tite Poulette, that this house
was to go to her and "the little one." In such fashion did this ancient residence
come to be called "Madame John's Legacy." But, to continue Cable's tale, Madame
John failed to hold on to the legacy and, "with the fatal caution which characterizes
ignorance, she sold the property and placed the proceeds in a bank, which mᵬde
haste to fail," and took up her living quarters in the building at the southᵥ ᵦst
corner, which we will presently visit.

"Madame John's Legacy," pictured so often by artists of the pen, pencil, brush, and camera, has known more than twenty owners in the course of two centuries, and its age and origin has been variously estimated. At last, after careful and painstaking research the true history of the old home has been revealed and all doubt and conjecture as to its origin swept aside.

The first owner and probable builder was Jean Pascal, a ship's captain from Provence, France, who came to New Orleans on January 15, 1726, and was given this particular site by *La Compagnie des Indies,* John Law's celebrated Company of the West, when it was exercising control of the Louisiana colony. Engineer Broutin's map of the city in 1728 shows Captain Pascal's place as being on lot 92, and here it was that the mariner and his wife and daughter lived.

Another owner was René Beluche, a ship's captain whose *goélette corsaire, The Spy,* carried on its particular business in the Barataria section before the Laffite brothers appeared there. In 1783 the old Pascal residence was occupied by Don Manuel de Lanzos, his wife, and six daughters. While it is true that the first major conflagration of 1788 wiped out many of the homes in the heart of the city, Governor Miro's map shows that the flames in this direction stopped before including this house with the others that were reduced to embers.

Señor de Lanzos, his wife the Señora Gertrude Guerro, and Louise, Antoinette, Gertrude, Marie, Joachim, and Grégoire, their six comely daughters, called this brick and cypress house home until ten years after the coming of the Americans, for it was not sold by the widow until 1813.

Many others have owned "Madame John's Legacy" and the old house has well withstood the ravages of the elements, but it was not until 1925, when Mrs. I. I. Lemann purchased the house made famous by Cable's fiction, that all fears for its possible demolition were set at rest. She saw to its preservation, and undoubtedly the spirit of Captain Jean Pascal was made glad. "Madame John's Legacy" is now owned by the Louisiana State Museum.

Across the street from "Madame John's Legacy" are two old one-story structures, interesting examples of early-day construction, whose exteriors display their age.

613 DUMAINE ST.—This small *casa* and the corner building adjoining were the property of Honoré Landreaux, a wealthy merchant, and were standing in 1803.

627-629 DUMAINE ST.—Long the home of Françoise Aubert, widow of Pierre Veillon, who acquired the property on March 15, 1790, when the house was undoubtedly erected.

FLEITAS BUILDING   841 ROYAL ST.

The massive three-story building at the southwest corner of Royal and Dumaine streets is one of many structures in the Old Square that belies its appearance in that it is older than it looks. Built in 1826 by Mme Marie Guenard, widow of Domingo Fleitas, a prominent merchant of the old town, it has housed a number of important commercial concerns but the structure will prove of greater interest to many because it was selected by George W. Cable to house three of his most appealing fictional characters.

Here it was that the writer domiciled 'Tite Poulettte and her mother, Zalli, the "Madame John" whose "legacy" we have just visited. Those who have read the story will recall that Kristian Koppig, the rosy-faced, beardless Dutchman, from the window of a cottage opposite saw "a building which still stands, flush with the street, a century old. Its big, round-arched windows in a long, second story row, are walled up, and two or three from time to time have had smaller windows let into them, with odd little latticed peep-holes in their batten shutters." These features led Cable to "guess that it is a remnant of the Spanish Barracks, whose extensive structure fell by government sale into private hands a long time ago."

In the good old days of duelling, and bagatelle-clubs, and theatre-balls, there lived in that portion of this house partly overhanging the archway, so Cable wrote, "a palish, handsome woman, by the name—or going by the name—of Madame John." There you have the character, a figment of Cable's gifted imagination, and here you have the very building in which Cable admirers claim he housed the attractive looking woman. Here it was, you will recall if you have read "'Tite Poulette," that a cigarbox filled with sand fell from a window ledge upon the head of the persistent and sinister manager of the *Salle de Condé*, where the octoroon balls were held.

KRISTIAN KOPPIG'S COTTAGE   707 DUMAINE ST.

Having seen "Madame John's Legacy" and the home of Zalli and 'Tite Poulette it is most appropriate that we inspect the cottage opposite in which the love-smitten young Hollander, Kristian Koppig, lived. The one-story plastered-brick cottage, the second house from Royal, is distinguished from every other house in the Quarter by its high front that is filled at the top by red, half-round Spanish tiles, looking like a sliced honeycomb. These partly hide the single dormer window from which Cable averred the young Dutchman watched for a glimpse of 'Tite Poulette, who turned out to be "a Spaniard's daughter" and not the child of a quadroon.

Whether or not a love-smitten Hollander ever called this cottage home we do not know; what we do know is that this small building is one of the old-timers of the Vieux Carré, and that it was built in 1800 by a doughty Spanish soldier, Don Joachim de la Torre, described as *el capitàn commandmant actuellement, Major de Brigade de Garde au service de sa Majesté le Roi d'Espagne*, and captain of engineers, in the act that recorded his purchase of the site from Barthelemy Lafon, the surveyor. Search as we may through the long list of subsequent owners, we do not find a single name that even sounds like Koppig. But that is no reason, is it, why we should not name it, as Cable did, "Kristian Koppig's Cottage"?

MILTENBERGER HOMES   900-914 ROYAL ST.

Bulking large against smaller buildings on the downtown river corner of Royal and Dumaine streets are three sturdy three-story red-brick buildings that housed, a century ago, the distinguished Miltenberger family of New Orleans. Originally, the corner site had on it the modest home of Dr. Christian Milten-Berger, as the name was originally spelled, and his wife, she who had been Mlle Marie Mercier. The physician served in the Battle of New Orleans as a surgeon attached to Major Plauché's contingent of Creoles.

In November of 1838 the Widow Miltenberger contracted with Rice & Tibbits, a firm of builders, to erect three buildings on the corner to be ready for occupancy the following June. The new houses, which cost $29,176, became the homes of the three Miltenberger sons—Gustave being given the corner house, Aristides occupying the middle residence, while Alphonse assumed ownership of the one at 910 Royal, which differs from those of his brothers by having a bay abutting on the spacious side courtyard.

THE KOHN BUILDINGS   916-924 ROYAL ST.

Immediately adjoining the Miltenberger courtyard is a triple-brick building erected during that hectic period in the life of the Old Square when houses sprouted like mushrooms after a summer shower. But, unlike that fungus growth, these buildings of the golden 1830s have defied time although the tide of business flowed in the opposite direction. Joachim Kohn, a banker of some repute in the old town, in September of 1838 entered into a contract with John Gilchrist Boyd to erect the buildings.

THE CORNSTALK FENCE   915 ROYAL ST.

The unique cast-iron fence that encloses this garden is of unusual interest to visitors whose attentions have been focused on the wrought- and cast-iron work that adorns so many of the balconies on practically every old building of note in the Vieux Carré.

The design of this cast-iron fence simulates growing cornstalks entwined with morning glories. In the golden 1830s, when cast iron began to take the place of wrought iron on balconies, it was quite the fashion to accent the illusion of growing plants cast in iron by coloring them in natural colors. This fence has been kept painted through the years: the stalks have been painted green, the ears of corn made yellow, while each morning-glory trumpet has been colored a heavenly blue. To the design of the gate has been added a broad-winged butterfly and, at the bottom, a spray of holly leaves.

The original home, since destroyed by fire, was owned by Dr. Joseph Secondo Biamanti, who had purchased the property from François Arsène Blanc on September 4, 1834. Old acts show that Blanc purchased this site in 1826 from Judge François Xavier Martin, the famed jurist and author of the first *History of Louisiana*. Judge Martin acquired the property ten years before and it remained his home for a decade.

The fence was cast in 1859 by the Wood & Perot Philadelphia iron foundry, shipped by boat to New Orleans, and erected on this site shortly after Antoinette Biamanti became the wife of Robert W. Ogden.

One other such fence in New Orleans encloses the beflowered courtyard at the corner of Prytania and Fourth streets in uptown New Orleans' famed Garden District.

WHERE JACKSON WAS FINED   919 ROYAL ST.

Adjoining the colorful cornstalk fence is the old courthouse in which United States District Judge Dominick Hall fined General Jackson $1,000 for being in contempt of his court. This fine was levied upon the "Saviour of New Orleans" a few weeks after he had beaten off the invading British army.

After the triumph of the battle of January 8, in spite of rumors that peace had been declared, "Old Hickory" kept alive his martial law, much to the indignation of a number of the Creole element. Louis Louaillier, a member of the legislature, published a lengthy communication in a newspaper bitterly criticizing Jackson. The general ordered the writer arrested and when Judge Hall issued a writ of *habeas corpus,* Jackson banished the judge from the city. When official news came that peace had been declared between the United States and Great Britain and Jackson declared his martial law ended, Judge Hall returned, reopened his court, ordered the victor of the famous battle before him, found him guilty of contempt of court, and fined him a round thousand dollars.

The original building was built during the Spanish regime as the first King's School to be erected in Louisiana, and was only one story high and covered by a roof of half-round red Spanish tile. It remained so for many years until sold by presidential proclamation on August 5, 1825. In the late 1880s the present structure was built on the foundations of the old Spanish schoolhouse.

GENERAL BEAUREGARD'S HOME   934 ROYAL ST.

Louisiana's contribution to the Confederacy in the Civil War, aside from the thousands of sons who fell in that great fratricidal strife, was General P. G. T. Beauregard, who on an April morning in 1861, ordered the guns of Charleston to open fire on Fort Sumter and thus begin that bitter four-year struggle. He was known as the "Great Creole" and aside from firing the first shot of the war, was the victor at the Battle of Bull Run and recognized as an able warrior and engineer— but Jefferson Davis hated him, and the Creole from Louisiana was forced to eat out his heart playing second fiddle to officers he outranked in ability . . . a pathetic "lost soldier in a lost cause."

Broken, disappointed, bitter, the "Great Creole" returned to New Orleans to doff his general's uniform of gray for the habiliments of private life. His wife had died while he was at the front, and he and his son during the winter of 1866-67 lived in rented apartments at old 279 Chartres Street, opposite the Ursulines' Convent, while the hero of Shiloh looked for a job. He got one, the presidency of a little railroad, 206 miles long, running from New Orleans to Canton, Mississippi. The road lasted long enough to be gobbled up by a larger railroad and Beauregard was again seeking work.

Cast-iron decoration over gateway to court at 934 Royal St.

In 1867 he moved into this fine old residence, now 934 Royal Street, and here he lived with his son René and a widowed older sister for more than eight years.

The entrance to the courtyard of the Royal Street mansion has an interesting bit of cast-iron work over the doorway. It is the so-called "lovebird" design, having a pair of doves on either side of a bowl of fruit, said to be the only example of its kind left in New Orleans, although it had been a favorite and popular design with those who demanded cast-iron decorations on their balconies.

Jean Gleises, a wheelwright of the early days who deserted the making of wagon wheels for the business of constructing buildings and thereby accumulated a healthy fortune, built this mansion and left it to his daughter Athalie.

As we continue down Royal Street on our sight-seeing promenade we will pass a number of century-old combination business and residential structures, none having sufficient historical interest to be singled out for particular attention.

At the southeast corner of Royal and St. Philip is a store which occupies a building erected in 1842.

As we cross the street we can glance to our left and observe the St. Philip Street school which occupies the site of the third oldest theatre in New Orleans, *Théâtre de la rue Saint-Philippe*, erected in 1808.

The building on the northeast corner of St. Philip and Royal is of interest for the grapevine design of its cast-iron balcony railings. It was erected August 23, 1832, by Honoré Landreaux, Jr.

The large building diagonally opposite on the southwest corner was built in 1830 by Marc Fauché Cougot. For many years it was occupied by the cotton commission firm of Gordon, Forstall & Co. Alexander Gordon was the husband of Anne Bakewell, and her sister was Mrs. John James Audubon.

"MADAME DELICIEUSE"   1027 ROYAL ST.

Those familiar with Cable's characters found in his exquisite stories that so truly depict the old folk of old New Orleans will be interested in the house at 1027 Royal Street. To quote from Lafcadio Hearn's account of his wanderings in the ancient thoroughfares of the Vieux Carré to locate the homes of Cable's fictional folk: "The visitor who follows the east side of Royal street might notice on the opposite side an elegant and lofty red brick mansion, with a deep archway piercing its *rez-de-chaussée* to the courtyard which offers a glimpse of rich foliage whenever the *porte cochère* is left ajar. This is the residence of 'Madame Délicieuse;' and worthy of that honor, it seems, with its superb tiara of green verandas. A minute two-story cottage squats down beside it—a miniature shop having tiny show-windows that project like eyes. The cottage is a modern affair; but it covers the site of Doctor Mossy's office, which, you know, was of lemon-yellow Creole construction, roofed with red tiles."

We can be interested in this alleged residence of the beautiful Madame Délicieuse for, even if the heroine of Cable's tender romance was an imaginary creature, the builder of the edifice was quite real. He was Patrick Macnamara, born in Ireland, as might be suspected, who married Marguerite Judith Chauvin de Léry des Islets. After marrying into such a prominent Louisiana Creole family as the des Islets, it is small wonder that Macnamara became a "Count."

DOCTOR MOSSY'S OFFICE
1026-1030 ROYAL ST.

Despite the fact that author Cable placed the office of the diminutive Doctor Mossy next door to the home of Madame Délicieuse, most of us prefer to imagine that the quiet little physician lived directly opposite in the tiny little one-story cottage that seemingly squats on the sidewalk. For it is old, very old, and although it has only one show-window "that projects like an eye," it is as dusty and disorderly as the establishment Cable described and the slate-covered roof slopes out over the sidewalk, as Doctor Mossy's did. The one-eyed show-window is protected by green batten shutters that evidently have not been removed for years.

Whether or not a Doctor Mossy ever occupied this relic of the days gone by, we can be interested in it from an antiquarian's standpoint for it was on July 7, 1790 that Enrique Mentzinger, captain of the Spanish army and adjutant of the Plaza, purchased the site from Elena Foucan and built the small structure. On July 6, 1803, just a few months before Spain's banner gave way to the stars and stripes of the Americans, *El Capitan* Mentzinger sold the cottage to Antonio Maria Tanguin. Subsequent owners have been many, and one thing is evident—here is one building of the Old Square that is as old as it looks.

CASA LALANDE
620 URSULINES ST.

At the next corner we should turn to our right, in the direction of the river, so we may inspect an interesting and very old Spanish *casa*, to be recognized instantly by the fan-shaped affair of pointed spikes on the ancient wrought-iron balcony *grillage*, the *garde de frise* that keeps possible intruders from entering the second-story windows. This *casa* was the old home of a celebrated family of old New Orleans, the de la Lande de Ferrières. Just when Nicolas Louis de Lalande erected this typical home is not quite certain. What we do know is that he was murdered on his own doorstep by a pirate and that his heirs sold the *casa* to Eugene Fortier in 1818.

The Lalande *casa* is typical Spanish construction having a central hallway with spacious living rooms opening on it from either side, and in the rear is the largest patio to be found in the Vieux Carré.

STREET OF BALCONIES   1101-1141 ROYAL ST.

Upon our return to Royal Street our attention is instantly caught by the row of houses on the left-hand side of the thoroughfare and their balconies covered with cast-iron lace and twining vines growing from the flower boxes and pots that line the galleries. These houses were all erected at one time by the forerunner in New Orleans of what we now denominate homestead and building and loan associations. This particular company, headed by Jules Mossy and operating under the name of *La Compagnie des Architectes,* purchased the entire site and in the winter of 1831-32 built the houses and sold them individually at public auction.

GALLIER'S RESIDENCE   1132 ROYAL ST.

On May 19, 1857, James Gallier, Jr., purchased the lot upon which this residence stands and built the present home. In the history of architecture in New Orleans the name Gallier shines bright, as bright as that of Latrobe, Lacarrière Latour, the de Pouilly and Dakin brothers, all having to their credit the designing of historic edifices that make the Vieux Carré so interesting to visitors. James Gallier and his son of the same name were designers of the old city hall, the Pontalba buildings, the original St. Charles Hotels, and many others. The cast-iron balcony railings, designed to simulate rosebuds, are most interesting. The house has been beautifully restored and is open to the public for tours.

"THE HAUNTED HOUSE"   1140 ROYAL ST.

The three-story building at the southeast corner of Royal and Governor Nicholls street, to some the most famous private residence in old New Orleans, gained its eerie title, "The Haunted House," from an oft-repeated tale in which spirits of tortured slaves clank their chains during the midnight hours in remembrance of awful punishment meted out to them by their mistress—a high-bred lady of old New Orleans who had been charged with finding an uncanny delight in dealing inhumanly with her slaves.

Like all such tales, the story has grown in ferocity through its countless retellings and the probabilities are that even the original story of over a century ago was a gross exaggeration. It now appears that the mistress of this home was the first victim of yellow journalism in this country and that she was far from being the "fiend" tradition has labelled, or should we say, libelled her. The facts of this "strange true story" are as follows.

The traditional tales of the Vieux Carré have it that this house was built in 1780 by two brothers, Jean and Henri de Remarie, and that such guests as Marshal Michel Ney, Napoleon's famous commander; the duc d'Orléans, later, Louis Philippe, king of France; and the Marquis de Lafayette have slept in this mansion. But we are compelled to make the pertinent observations that Marshal Ney never came to Louisiana, that Louis Philippe was here in 1798, and that Lafayette visited New Orleans in 1825—yet the "Haunted House" was not built until 1832!

There are those who denounce historical accuracy when it destroys fallacious tradition . . . those who claim that a good story must never be sacrificed and crucified on the cross of truth. Much as one admires the colorful traditions of old New Orleans, our mission is to give a factual history of the landmarks of the Vieux Carré. So, to stick to fact, we must point out that the lots upon which the "Haunted House" stands were purchased by Mme Louis Lalaurie, September 12, 1831, from Edmond Soniat du Fossat, and the house then built was not ready for occupancy until the spring of 1832. As it was part of the tract given the Ursuline nuns, this was the first, and only, house built on this particular site.

Mme Lalaurie was one of five children born to Louis Barthélemy Chevalier de Macarty and Marie Jeanne Lovable, two who stood high in the social life of old New Orleans. One of their daughters was christened Marie Delphine Macarty. She first married, on June 11, 1800, Don Ramon de Lopez y Angula, the ceremony being performed in the Saint Louis Cathedral by Luis de Penalver y Cardenas, the first bishop of the diocese of Louisiana, and the marriage certificate was signed by the celebrated Fray Antonio de Sedella. The husband was described in this document as a *Caballero de la Royal de Carlos,* Intendent of the Provinces, a native of the community of Regno, Galicia, Spain, and the legitimate son of his Lordship Don José Antonio de Lopez y Angula and Doña Ana Fernande de Angula, daughter of Doña Francisca Borja Endecis.

Shortly after the Louisiana Purchase, on March 26, 1804, Delphine Macarty's husband was recalled to the court of Spain, the letter carrying this royal command stating that the young Spanish officer was "to take his place at court as befitting his new position." At this time Don Ramon was consul general for Spain in this new American territory. While in Havana, en route to Madrid, Don Ramon suddenly died and a few days later his daughter was born in the Cuban city. This infant was baptized Marie Delphine Borja Lopez y Angula de Candelaria, but she became best known in later years as "Borquita," meaning "little Borja," from the fact that she was named after her father's grandmother.

Left a widow, Delphine Macarty and her baby daughter returned to New Orleans. Four years later, in 1808, she again married, choosing for her husband a prominent banker, merchant, lawyer, and legislator named Jean Blanque, a native of Béarn who had come to Louisiana with Prefect Laussat in 1803. At the time of his marriage, June 16, 1808, Blanque purchased the residence at 409 Royal Street and in this home Delphine became the mother of four other children: Marie Louise Pauline, Louise Marie Laure, Marie Louise Jeanne, and Jean Pierre Paulin Blanque. In that stylish Royal Street home or in the "Villa Blanque," a charming country place fronting the Mississippi River just below the city limits, Delphine Macarty Blanque divided her time, both places being frequented by the socially elect.

Jean Blanque died in 1816, and Delphine Macarty remained a widow until June 12, 1825, when she again married. Her third husband was Dr. Leonard Louis Nicolas Lalaurie, a native of Villeneuse-sur-Lot, France, who came to New Orleans to establish a practice. Borquita, the daughter by her mother's first marriage, became the wife of Placide Forstall, member of a distinguished Louisiana family, and Jeanne Blanque married Charles Auguste de Lassus, only child of Don Carlos de

Lassus, former governor of Upper Louisiana, and later governor of the Baton Rouge post of West Florida when they were under Spanish rule.

The Lalaurie mansion was erected in 1832 and for the next two years was the scene of many fashionable affairs, for the Lalauries entertained on an elaborate plan. On the afternoon of April 10, 1834, an aged cook set fire to the house during the absence of her mistress. When neighbors rushed into the mansion to fight the fire and try to save the furniture and other valuables, slaves were found chained in their quarters. Although the fire was extinguished, the indignation of those who found the helpless slaves blazed high and a newspaper editor, Jerome Bayon, of the *Bee,* published a heated account of the happening and quoted those who had investigated the Lalaurie slave quarters. This newspaper account roused public indignation to such a pitch that on April 15 a mob, led by irresponsibles, charged the house and began to wreck it. The rowdies were finally dispersed by a company of United States regulars who had been called out by a helpless sheriff.

During the excitement Madame Lalaurie and her husband took to their carriage and, with her faithful Creole black coachman Bastien on the box, swept through the howling, cursing rabble and, with the horses lashed to the full gallop, made her way out of the city. It is supposed the carriage reached Bayou St. John where a lake craft was secured, for on April 21, 1834, the Lalauries were in Mandeville, across Lake Pontchartrain, at the home of Louis Coquillon. There Madame Lalaurie signed a power-of-attorney placing her son-in-law Placide Forstall in charge of her affairs, while her husband signed a similar document in favor of his wife's other son-in-law, Auguste de Lassus. From Mandeville the Lalauries made their way to Mobile, where a ship took them to France.

Neither Delphine nor her husband ever returned to New Orleans. She remained in Paris, living there honored and respected in spite of the lurid tales that lived after her in New Orleans. Following her death on December 7, 1842, her body was secretly returned to New Orleans and buried in St. Louis No. 1 Cemetery.

The Lalaurie mansion was sold to various owners but the tale that it was "haunted" and the midnight rendezvous for ghosts grew in the telling as only such stories can grow. The principal "ghost" is, according to the most frequently quoted tale, that of a little girl slave who, to escape the whip of her mistress, climbed to the roof and jumped to her death into the courtyard below. Another tale, equally untrue, was that the mistress of the mansion buried all her victims in the courtyard well. The general impression that the place was haunted was sufficient to keep superstitious blacks from passing the house after nightfall.

In the days of the Reconstruction following the Civil War, the old Lalaurie mansion became the Lower Girls' School. During the government of the carpetbaggers, whites and blacks were taught in the same rooms until the formation of "The White League" in 1874, when the white element marched on the house and expelled the black pupils. In the 1880s the mansion became a conservatory of music. No matter who has lived in it since, or the manner of business that was carried on in the ground-floor stores, the name "haunted" has clung to it in spite of the testimony of those inhabiting the place that ghosts have never disturbed their slumbers.

Tradition has it that the handsome entrance door "was hammered out of iron by the slaves Madame Lalaurie kept shackled to the anvil." This must be taken with several generous pinches of salt, for the door is not of iron but wood and the decorations on it were not carved but put on by appliqué, a sort of plastic wood applied and formed as a sculptor would lay on his modeling clay. These ornamentations show, in the lower oblong panel, Phoebus in his chariot, lashing his griffins. Scattered over the door are urns, flowers, trumpet-blowing angels, a beribboned lyre, an American eagle bearing on its breast the shield of the Union, leaves, scrolls, and whatnots—a marvelous example of some unknown craftsman's art. To save the door from the knives of souvenir-hunters, one owner painted it a dingy brown-black.

George W. Cable's Strange Stories of Louisiana, *and Judge Henry C. Castellanos'* New Orleans As It Was, *contain full accounts of the Lalaurie episode. My account, differing in many respects from those of these earlier writers, is based on recently found documents, notarial acts, and family documents.*

CASA CORREJOLLES   715 GOVERNOR NICHOLLS ST.

We can leave Royal Street for a minute and take a few steps into ancient Hospital Street (for even today there are many who rebel against the modern name given the old thoroughfare) to inspect two architectural oddities. On the downtown side at No. 715 a most interesting example of the wrought-iron artisan's work can be seen on the balcony of an old home built by Gabriel Correjolles in 1834, when he also erected the adjoining corner building which is diagonally opposite the Lalaurie mansion.

"SPANISH STABLES"   724 GOVERNOR NICHOLLS ST.

Opposite the old Correjolles home is a very interesting construction, frequently designated as the former "Spanish Cavalry Barracks," although the arched stable stalls, with living quarters for the riders or drivers above them, were built thirty years after the Spanish soldiers had left New Orleans.

These sturdy arches or *portales,* the whole forming an elongated "U" that reaches deep into the center of the square, were built in 1834 by Judge Gallien

Wrought-iron balcony railing at 715 Gov. Nicholls St.

Cast-iron design on the gallery at 1125 Royal St.

Préval for the purpose of a commercial livery stable, and were identical with a like construction at 1122 Royal Street, formerly occupied by an old seltzer water factory. Cable, Hearn, and other early writers claimed these were the old Spanish Barracks, but the Royal Street "barracks," like Judge Préval's stables in *rue de l'Hôpital,* were built long after the Royal Horse of Spain clattered out of the city. Unfortunately, fact and tradition in the Old Square do not always dovetail. The stables have been restored and adapted for use as residential apartments.

"MADAME DELPHINE'S"   1212-1214 ROYAL ST.

If you are interested in the supposed residences of the supposed folk found in Cable's stories of *Old Creole Days,* do not neglect to observe Nos. 1212-1214 Royal Street. No one who has ever read "Madame Delphine" can readily forget the author's description of "the small, low, brick house of a story and a half, set out upon the sidewalk, as weather-beaten and mute as an aged beggar fallen asleep." This was the house, so claimed Lafcadio Hearn, that Cable selected as the residence of Delphine Carraze, the quadroon who lied to give her near-white daughter happiness.

AUDUBON'S FIRST STUDIO   706 BARRACKS ST.

Just a step off Royal Street, in the ancient *rue du Quartier,* is a low brick house that at one time was the home of a gay Spaniard named Don Juan Puich. Here it was, in 1821, that a struggling, unknown artist, whose consuming passion was that of depicting birds on paper, rented a room and in it established his first studio in New Orleans. The bird man, who then only dreamed of future greatness, was John James Audubon, the talented Franco-American whose bronze statue now occupies a commanding site in a great park which also bears his name. Long considered a native of Louisiana, Audubon was not born in this state, but in it he drew the majority of the bird portraits that afterwards brought him world acclaim. From February 22 until June 20, 1821, Audubon and his young assistant, Joseph R. Mason, lived in this inconspicuous little brick house. He left it when given the opportunity to go to a Louisiana bird paradise, West Feliciana Parish, where the birds sang as nowhere else and where the budding naturalist learned much of the habits of the brilliant little citizens of the air. Audubon's second studio, "the little house in Dauphine Street," is described in the chapter "Down Bourbon Street."

Along the Esplanade

ONLY A BLOCK FURTHER yawns the dreamy magnificence of once-upon-a-time aristocratic Esplanade Avenue, with its broad, central neutral ground of grass all shadow-flecked by a double line of trees. It is there that *rue Royale* originally terminated, the Esplanade forming the boundary line of the lower side of the Old Square.

We can turn along it, in the direction of the river, to continue a scheduled sightseeing promenade up Chartres Street. Or we can, while we are in this former aristocratic neighborhood, inspect a few of the palatial residences that were, just over a century ago, the homes of the elite, the well-to-do who erected splendid edifices.

A sight-seeing saunter along the Esplanade will permit us to inspect a few handsome old residences owned by the socially prominent Orleanians of over a century ago. The Esplanade was originally called a *promenade publique* by the authorities when the city sold the properties on the outer side of an oblique line that bisected the original squares of the lower section of the Old Town. On this line were laid the old ramparts that stretched from Fort San Carlos to Fort San Juan. It was a number of years after the American occupation, and during the boom days of the late 1830s, that this part of the Vieux Carré became a stylish residential area. If we elect to start our Esplanade tour at Decatur Street, the first old building to command our attention is the following.

524 ESPLANADE—Known today as the Cusachs home from the fact that Gaspar Cusachs, who purchased it in 1893, was president of the Louisiana Historical Society for many years. A student of the history of the city and state, his collection of documents, books, portraits, and other historical relics was a noted one, many items being bequeathed to the Louisiana State Museum upon his death and now on display in the Cabildo. The old residence, which has been extensively repaired, appears to have had its foundations laid in 1810 by its first owner, Laurent Buzard, and, if this is true, it is the oldest structure in the Esplanade.

544 ESPLANADE—The massive building at the corner of Chartres Street was built

Detail of cast-iron balcony railing at Royal and Esplanade

in 1853 by François Gras, who sold the place six years later to Claude Tiblier. During the Civil War the mansion was occupied by many of the socially elect and in 1875 it became the home of Michel Lion.

600-604-606 ESPLANADE—These three once imposing triple-story brick residences were built in 1832 by Henry R. Denis, a prominent attorney, as an investment. In 1835 the center structure was sold to Judge Alonzo Morphy, father of the celebrated chess champion Paul Morphy. The residence at 606 was sold at the same time to Michel Doradou Bringier, a wealthy Ascension Parish planter, who presented it to his daughter Louise when she married Martin Gordon, Jr. In 1850 the side lot was purchased and the original building enlarged by the addition of the prominent bay now abutting on the courtyard, which "in the days before the war" was a delightful and beautiful garden. Like many another splendid Esplanade residence, the old Bringier mansion gradually fell into sad decay but it has been restored by successive owners.

638 ESPLANADE—The diminutive structure at the corner of Royal Street which appears by its construction to be very old dates back in the records to the year 1828, when Tedro Robert sold the tiny home to Don Joaquin Diaz, who disposed of it in 1843 to Leon M. Ximeno.

704 ESPLANADE—On the western corner of Royal Street is the most pretentious structure in the Esplanade, a home which has long attracted the attention of home folk as well as sightseers from out of town. The solid construction of the mansion, its courtyard on the Royal Street side, and the garden filled with flowers have long singled it out as exceptional. However, to some, it is the design of the cast iron on a balcony, which surrounds the residence on three sides, that holds one's attention ... for the dancing cupid (or is it the infant Bacchus doing the original bacchanal?) is as unique as it is artistic and is the only design of its kind in a city famous for unique iron balcony decorations. It was cast in Saarbrucken, Germany, and shipped to New Orleans. The design is said to have been copied from an engraving

by Albrecht Dürer, the noted German painter and engraver. The mansion was built in 1856 by John Gauche, a crockery merchant, and remained his home until he sold it in 1882. The Gauche home was restored in 1938 and again in 1969.

714 ESPLANADE—Adjoining the Gauche residence is the mansion erected by André Brousseau about the same time John Gauche was putting up his building. Later the William G. Vincent, Pierre Ader, and Jean Jule Aldigé families owned and lived in it.

730-740 ESPLANADE—Set well back in a garden, a beflowered spot hidden from those who may pass by a high brick wall, is a fine old mansion that was once the home of Eliza Wilkins, the widow of Alverez Fisk, who with his brother Abijah came to New Orleans from Maine to make their fortunes. If we open the ornamental iron gate, which once had a design of an American eagle bearing on its breast the shield of the Union, we will better observe the brick house that sits well back in the spacious garden. This building was erected soon after Citye Rose Alverez sold the site to Alverez Fisk's widow on May 4, 1855. The corner building, which is much more pretentious, was built by Edward A. Fisk in 1870. It has become through the years one of the many McDonogh schools, No. 28; it was remodeled in 1889, and later was sold to the French 14th of July Society. The building is now an apartment house. The Fisk brothers, sons of a Maine state farmer, never occupied either of these two homes. As a hobby they collected books, and at their death left the library to the city which formed the nucleus of New Orleans' present public library system.

810-812 ESPLANADE—These twin residences were built in 1832 by Louis Thimelé Caire, a prominent notary, soon after he purchased the site from the widow of Pierre Dufour of Opelousas.

820 ESPLANADE—This old mansion was built by J. B. Guerin in 1828.

824-830 ESPLANADE—This curious old brick building set in a large plot of ground was erected in 1839 by Emile Sainet, a commission merchant.

906 ESPLANADE—The mansion was erected by George Legendre, an attorney, in 1831 and remained his residence until 1838. The cast-iron grilles in the garret windows are unique decorations and typical of that period.

908 ESPLANADE—This is one of the finer residences of this aristocratic thoroughfare which has been restored to its former grandeur. It was erected in 1835 by Céleste Destrehan, who was then separated from her husband, Prosper Marigny, the son of the famed Bernard Marigny, and became one of the socially prominent mansions of this section of the city. After her marriage to Alexandre Graihle she sold the property to Joseph Oscar Robelot, in 1839, for $20,000.

926 and 932 ESPLANADE—These two residences were built in 1839 by Jacques Dupré of Opelousas, Saint Landry Parish, a wealthy planter who made heavy investments in New Orleans property, especially in the stylish Esplanade.

938 ESPLANADE—Now occupied by a veterinary hospital, this building was the first investment made by Jacques Dupré, who erected it in 1830.

1002 ESPLANADE—This corner building was erected by the N. O. Building and Improvement Co., soon after the site was purchased on April 16, 1834. It was sold in 1838 to Jean Baptiste Dupiere. When sold to Joseph Dusuau it was a two-story mansion and it appears the new owner added an extra story.

1016 ESPLANADE—The ancient brick residence, fashioned somewhat on the lines of a feudal castle, was built in 1838 by Sampson Blossman. Many others have owned this old residence including Edward Pilsbury, a one-time mayor; William Henry Haynes; Joaquin Viosca, Jr.; Jacques Vitaut, a prominent jeweler; Mrs. Rosa C. Solari, widow of Jacques Koehl; and not so many years ago it housed the Hemlock exchange of the telephone company.

Cast-iron panel and knocker on door at 1125 Royal St.

As we finish the sight-seeing exploration along the former stylish Esplanade, we can turn into Burgundy Street and, by walking a short block to Barracks Street, inspect one of the mystery buildings of the Old Square.

"MORRO CASTLE"   1003 BARRACKS ST.

A square, granite-faced building at the northwest corner of Burgundy and Barracks streets, known to the neighborhood folk as "Morro Castle," has long been a mystery structure. Many eerie tales have been told of its past and its present, startling stories have been fabricated as to its genesis and, as its past has been shrouded in conjecture, like many another structural enigma, it has been accused of being the favorite rendezvous of ghosts. One prevalent belief is that this rather unprepossessing square pile of masonry and granite was built to quarter the troops of Carlos IV when the Dons ruled Louisiana and, consequently, this was "the old Spanish *cuartel* or barracks."

Another tale, one that has found itself into print on more than one occasion, goes as follows. Just before the outbreak of the Civil War two mysterious Frenchmen arrived in New Orleans and, finding a quantity of granite left over from the construction of the Custom House, purchased the stone, erected this square structure, and christened it "Morro Castle." No one knew the names of these two mysterious Frenchmen, so runs the tradition. One tale had it they were brothers. Another accused them of being bankers. Whether brothers, bankers, or both, their names were never divulged—but they built this place of superfluous Custom House granite blocks and g-g-g-ghosts walked through its corridors.

That a square building should have been christened "Morro Castle" at once arouses suspicion. Those who know their Spanish know that *morro* in the musical language of Castile means "round"—and the building is as square as a die. Research reveals the following facts about one of the really odd buildings of the Vieux Carré.

In the year 1829 Denis Prieur, then mayor of New Orleans, sold this corner lot to the Reverend Louis Muni, rector of Saint Louis Cathedral. In September of 1831 Father Muni sold the lots to Paul Pandelly, a well-known merchant who had married Euphrosine Dimitry, and in 1836 Mr. Pandelly engaged the services of an architect named Journot to draw plans for an edifice. Before the building could be finished, Pandelly found himself in financial difficulties and creditors foreclosed. In December of 1838 the "unfinished building of brick and granite" was sold to Pierre Soulé, noted attorney and diplomat, for $20,000. Soulé finished the construction, leased it to tenants and, in 1841, sold the "castle" to François Barthelemy Le Beau, a well-to-do planter.

The only mystery attached to this old building seems to be—why such a traditional history? There were no two French brothers, bankers or otherwise, connected with its construction. It was not built of granite left over from the construction of the Custom House because Collector Denis Prieur did not lay its cornerstone until

1849 and the customs building was not occupied until 1856—ten years after Pandelly's peculiar palace had been erected and filled with tenants! Whether it is haunted or not depends solely on whether or not *you* believe in ghosts.

This misnamed "Morro Castle" is worth a visit and inspection—it has a court-yard entered through a peculiarly zigzag corridor, and a fine stairway on the Burgundy Street side has a solid mahogany balustrade with solid copper newel-posts. Later purchasers of Pandelly's palace restored the place and converted its rooms into modern Frenchtown apartments.

A Walk Up Chartres Street

CHARTRES STREET, WHICH we will choose for our walk back, or "uptown," is every bit as interesting, as picturesque, and as old, if not older, than *rue Royale*. Here, in what was the principal commercial street of the old city, as in Royal, the principal residential street, one will miss many interesting sights if he walks along its narrow *banquettes* with eyes kept on the level of the street. We should halt, now and then, and inspect the many balconies which hang over the footways, peer into doorways as we saunter by, even halt and enter some of the dark, tunnel-like corridors just beyond the heavy wooden *porte cochères*, for they positively invite us to bright courtyards which lie beyond.

From the ramparts that lined the lower edge of the Old Square to the Cathedral, this street was originally *rue de Condé* and was so called until 1856, when the city authorities named its entire length Chartres Street. We must walk a block from the Esplanade before we come to the first houses of interest.

1235 CHARTRES STREET—At the southwest corner of Chartres and Barracks streets is an old, very old, two-story building erected in 1824 by François Bougère, a Saint Charles Parish planter, soon after he acquired the site from the United States government.

1227-1229-1231 CHARTRES STREET—The three buildings adjoining the old Bougère *casa* are typical three-story structures erected during the 1830s by builders of New Orleans. They were erected in 1835 by Manuel Lizardi, one of three brothers composing the Cuban firm of Lizardi Hermanos, soon after the wealthy commission merchant acquired the site from James Hopkins.

As we continue up Chartres Street we find, as we cross old Hospital Street (now Governor Nicholls), an assemblage of ancient houses that seem to huddle together like a group of wearied cattle lashed by a storm. They all date after the time, in 1824, when the Ursuline nuns decided to move their activities from their original convent to a new one below the city. The original area granted the nuns included four of the present city squares, those bounded by Decatur and Royal and Ursulines and Barracks streets. With the exception of the area immediately about the convent the remainder of their holdings was divided into building lots and sold to citizens. As these sales took place between 1825 and 1828, none of the structures in these squares can claim an age beyond those years.

The square we are now approaching is an historic one. On our left, just beyond the church, is the convent occupied by the Ursuline nuns in 1749, which gives it an age of more than two centuries. Directly opposite the convent is a structure which has long been an object of interest to every tourist who counts an exploration of the Vieux Carré the main event of his visit to New Orleans.

PAUL MORPHY'S BIRTHPLACE/LeCARPENTIER-BEAUREGARD-KEYES HOUSE   1113 Chartres St.

It was in this house, facing the aged Ursulines' Convent, that Paul Charles Morphy, the American master of chess, was born. There may be doubt as to where chess originated, but there is no doubt that in this house on June 27, 1837, a boy was born who, before he was out of his teens, became America's chess master. Paul Morphy's career, while short, was brilliant and he became one of New Orleans' noted sons. His birthplace was built by his grandfather, Joseph LeCarpentier, a noted auctioneer of the old town who had purchased the site, which then included grounds to the corner of Ursulines Street, on January 4, 1825, at the time the Ursulines abandoned their old convent for a new nunnery. On August 11, 1826, he entered into a contract with James Lambert to build on this lot a new home from designs drawn by Francisco Correjolles.

LeCarpentier's daughter, Louise Thérèse Félicite Thelcide, had married Alonzo Morphy, then a prominent attorney, and when the residence was completed February 1, 1827, the Morphys were invited to share the home and its spacious side garden. Here it was that little Paul was born. His history and that of his father has already been told in the description of 417 Royal Street.

Paul Morphy's birthplace (drawn by Catherine M. Howell)

In later years a local society purchased the old LeCarpentier mansion and, furnishing it with mementos of the distinguished Louisiana Confederate leader, General P. G. T. Beauregard (who resided here only six weeks during the winter of 1866-67 in rented rooms), rechristened it "Beauregard House" with the intention of making it a permanent memorial to "The Great Creole." General Beauregard's home at 934 Royal Street, where he lived from 1867 to 1875, has already been described.

Novelist Frances Parkinson Keyes lived in the house for many years. Today the foundation she created works to preserve the property. The house is open to the public for tours.

URSULINES' CONVENT   1114 Chartres St.

If we will stand on the gallery of Paul Morphy's birthplace we can leisurely inspect the venerable edifice directly opposite. Long supposed to be the first nunnery built in Louisiana and the oldest building in the Mississippi Valley, we find that this latter distinction belongs to a building in Dumaine Street better known as "Madame John's Legacy."

The Ursulines, who came to New Orleans on August 6, 1727, were the first of that order to establish themselves in what is now the United States. They were domiciled, while their first convent was being built, at Knolly's Ste. Reine concession at what is now Bienville and Chartres streets. These black-habited nuns conducted the first Catholic school in Louisiana, the first Indian and black school, and the first Catholic orphanage. In historic interest this venerable pile ranks with Saint Louis Cathedral. The construction of their convent was planned in 1727 but the cornerstone was not set in place until 1730 and it was July 17, 1734, before its doors were thrown open. This first convent, three stories high, was not constructed properly for its wall sunk and it became necessary to tear it down and build a second one, which was not completed until 1749.

Therefore, for almost two centuries the present building has been, in turn, a convent for girls, a school for Indians, a palace for the archbishop of the diocese, a meeting place for the Louisiana legislature, an academy for boys, a church presbytery, and the archival repository for the Archdiocese of New Orleans.

From 1749 to 1824 the devout disciples of Saint Ursula taught the daughters of the colonists in this structure and it was only abandoned by them because of the rise in the value of real estate around it. They then deemed it wise to dispose of the greater part of their property and establish a new convent two miles below the city. As the order owned three squares of property, the sale of all land not essential to the purposes of the convent brought the nuns a tidy sum with which to build their new convent and provided the growing city with a number of building lots. The Ursulines gave the convent to the presiding head of the Catholic church, the Abbé Dubourg, and he permitted a young French priest, Father Martial, to establish a school for boys in the building which heretofore had known only the presence of girls. The boys were instructed under the Lancastrian system and, while at first a successful venture, it soon proved a failure. The Louisiana legislature, which had been meeting in the old Orleans Ballroom following the destruction of the ancient French-built state house at Old Levee and Toulouse streets in 1828, occupied the old nunnery in 1831.

Later the convent was advanced to the dignity of an archbishopric and was later called the palace of Archbishop Blanc. In the pavement in front of the postern may still be seen the French designation *"Archevêché"* and on the cypress door of the postern is an interesting iron knocker. In 1899 a new archbishop's domicile was established on Esplanade Avenue.

The convent of the Ursulines was made over to the adjoining church building for use as a presbytery. This house of worship, Saint Mary's Italian Chruch, was erected in 1846, one end of the convent being demolished to permit the joining of the two buildings. The tale, frequently told, "that the heart of every archbishop of the diocese has been buried under the altar of Saint Mary's Church," has no foundation in fact.

JACKSON SQUARE

We are now arrived at the very heart of old New Orleans. The square space of green grass and waving trees facing the curved sweep of the Mississippi River was known from the time of the city's original settlement as the *Parade* or *Place d'Armes*. When the Spanish ruled the province and its capital city, this open space was called *Plaza de Armas*. Forty-eight years after the Louisiana Purchase, or in 1851, the old *Parade* was renamed for Andrew Jackson, hero of the Battle of New Orleans and seventh president of the United States, who bestrides a rearing bronze horse in the exact center of "Jackson Square."

This is probably the most historic spot in Louisiana. Many flags have caught the breeze high above the square of ground—first, the three golden lilies on the white banner of the House of Bourbon, designating the rule of Louis of France; next the golden castles and rampant red lions on the red and white quartered ensign of Spain, followed by the red and yellow striped pavilion of Hispanola when the bars

of Aragon were adopted in 1785 as the national ensign; the fourth flag was the tricolor of republican France, which waved over the square for only twenty short days; the fifth flag was an ensign of fifteen stars and fifteen stripes, telling all who could see its rippling folds that the infant United States had purchased Louisiana from the crafty Bonaparte for four cents an acre.

The Stars and Stripes rippled and waved over the ancient square for fifty-eight years before it was hauled down to make way for another banner—a strange flag it was, the "Lone Star" flag of the state of Louisiana. Representatives of the people, in convention assembled, dissolved the bonds that bound the state with the Union and joined the Confederacy. This Lone Star flag had thirteen stripes, which alternated blue, white, red, white, blue, etc.; the jack was red with a single large five-pointed star in its center. For a year this state flag flew side by side with the banner of the Confederacy. On April 25, 1862, Admiral David Glasgow Farragut, who as a barefoot boy had played in this very square, anchored the Union fleet off the old *Place d'Armes*. The next day the Louisiana Lone Star and the flag of the Confederacy were lowered and the Stars and Stripes again responded to the soft caresses of vagrant river breezes.

Thus has the square known seven differing flags representing five peoples and their governments.

In 1851, the old *Place d'Armes*, laid off by engineer Adrien de Pauger on March 5, 1721, and since that time theatre of many of Louisiana's most thrilling historical events, was transformed from a parade designed for the tramping of soldier feet to a beautiful garden. It was laid out with walks and formal *parterres* and re-christened with the name of the hero of the Battle of New Orleans. This rehabilitation and improvement of the old *Place* was undertaken by a society founded by Madame de Pontalba, whose red-brick apartment houses flank the square. She also made the largest contribution to the fund that erected the statue of Old Hickory and insisted that the ancient heart of New Orleans be renamed for General Jackson.

The Jackson statue is a unique piece of craftsmanship. It will be noted that Clark Mills, the sculptor, did not rely on rods or props beneath the front hooves of the bronze steed to keep it in its rearing posture. He succeeded in effecting a perfect balance without them. The bronze of horse and rider weighs more than 20,000 pounds, its cost was $30,000, and the memorial was unveiled February 9, 1856. It was a replica of the same statue in Washington, D.C., and in Nashville, Tennessee. The inscription, "The Union Must and Shall Be Preserved," was ordered cut in the granite base in 1862 by Ben Butler, the Yankee general who, Orleanians like to believe, stole all their grandmothers' silver spoons.

SAINT LOUIS CATHEDRAL

One of the notable landmarks of North America is the Saint Louis Cathedral, which faces what we now call Jackson Square and it, as did its two predecessors,

The Saint Louis Cathedral, as seen from Jackson Square—the heart of old New Orleans (drawn and copyrighted by Morris Henry Hobbs)

The appearance of the Cathedral in 1838 (redrawn from an old engraving)

looks out upon the crescent bend of the Mississippi River and the green grasses and trees in the ancient *Place d'Armes* where so many important events in the history of old New Orleans took place.

The present church dates from 1794 and is the third structure raised to the honor of and christened with the name of the patron saint of Bourbon France. Just when the first church was erected is not certain although it is known that a rude place of worship was hastily thrown up on the site soon after Bienville located his new seat of government for Louisiana. Whatever its form, whether an actual church or a converted *magasin,* the first church was swept away by the hurricane of September 12, 1722, which also demolished most of the other buildings erected by the colonists.

For several years the pious colonists worshipped in a house rented from one of the citizens. There were no pews or chairs and the more well-to-do colonists and officials went to church on Sundays and feast days with servants following with chairs. A new church was projected in 1724, but the edifice was not completed and dedicated until April 1727. This second church of Saint Louis was built of brick and wood, the outside walls covered with *adobe* plaster, and was counted then a splendid building. It had a tall tower and belfry with entrances on either side as well as a front doorway that looked upon the *Place d'Armes*. The church had a special seat for the governor and intendant, as well as for the members of the Superior Council and military officers. The other pews were auctioned off to the highest bidders, which led to contention and rivalry among the parishioners intent on securing the best pews. Father Raphael de Luxemburg, an energetic Capuchin, was the superior and pastor of the new church and in it were performed the marriage ceremonies for the poor and slaves as well as for the aristocrats. Here, too, were baptized the infants of the officials and the children of the workers and the slaves. Even in its early days the church of Saint Louis had an organ and a choir and, being the center of all life of the old town, official pronouncements were posted on the door of the house of worship.

This was the church of the early French settlers. When France gave Louisiana to Spain and the Dons came into possession of the city, repairs were made to the ancient structure of *briquette entre poteaux* (bricks between posts). In 1785 the pious flocked to the old church to witness, for the first time here, the functioning of a bishop when Padre Cyrillo de Barcelona, a Spanish friar, was elevated to the dignity of auxiliary bishop and the spiritual care of Louisiana was placed in his hands.

When the Good Friday fire of March 21, 1788, swept *Nueva Orléans*, 856 buildings, including the Church of Saint Louis, were reduced to smoldering ruins. To replace the house of worship a rich Andalusian, who had come to the newly possessed Spanish colony twenty years before a penniless *escribano*, unloosed his tightly held purse strings and offered to build a new house of God. The offer was accepted, but only after a great deal of bickering among the members of the *Illustrious Cabildo*, which so sorely tried the patience of Don Andres Almonester y Roxas, the former notary who had made the offer, that he was ready to withdraw the proposal. Some insight may be found of this quarrel in the proceedings of the Cabildo. On October 2, 1789, the entry states: "Attorney Don Valentine Robert Avart advised the Illustrious Council that the public sufferers had been disappointed by the promises of Don Andres Almonester, *alcalde de segundo voto* (junior judge), made after the fire and in public gatherings of the notables of the city, that he would repair the church damaged by the fire. The members of the Cabildo must know his desire about fulfilling his early promises and have it in writing."

The answer proved evasive, and on December 11 the members of the Cabildo decided to send Don Andres "a simple message . . . with the only purpose of asking him to kindly state plainly whether he has decided to reconstruct said parish church or not, so that, in view of his final answer, in case of unexpected refusal, we might have time to take other convenient steps toward the goal of such holy endeavor."

The next day, December 12, 1789, Don Almonester was again elected a junior judge and promised to "continue the work of rebuilding the church." A few months later, on March 18, 1790, Almonester was made Perpetual Commissioner and Royal Ensign of the Cabildo. This suggests that the church builder had insisted that some of his demands be met and that he only exchanged *pesos* from his huge purse for honors in the ruling body of province. He had previously built the Hospital of San Carlos de Caridad, the chapel for the Ursulines' Convent, and the Hospital of San Lazaro for lepers. After he had reconstructed the Saint Louis Church he asked that on every Saturday following his death that a mass should be said for the repose of his soul. There is a beautiful tradition, still to be found in the late writings about New Orleans, that every Saturday, at sunset, the cathedral bell is tolled in honor of the builder, and that masses are offered up for his soul—as Almonester had requested. This is no longer the practice and to many of the pious, it is a matter of real regret that masses "in perpetuity" have been allowed to lapse.

When Don Andres Almonester y Roxas died on April 26, 1798, he was buried in the parish cemetery. A year and a half later his remains were disinterred and sepulchred at the foot of the marble step of the altar of the Most Blessed Virgin of the Rosary of the Cathedral, under a large marble slab on which are inscribed his name, coat of arms, and a record of his life, his honors, and his deeds.

The new church erected by Don Andres, who not only supplied the necessary funds but supervised its construction, was a much larger and more impressive structure than the one burned. Although the work on the new *Iglesia San Luis* was begun in 1792, the edifice was not finished until 1794. When first erected it had two bell-topped hexagonal towers on each side of the facade, there was no central spire or tower, and the flat tile roof was edged with a balustrade and covered with flat and hollow tile. It cost Almonester 98,988 *pesos,* 1 1/2 *reales,* to build the church, according to Spanish court documents.

Hardly had the new church been completed, but not thrown open for devotions, than, on December 8, 1794, when the fete of the Immaculate Conception was being observed, another conflagration swept the city, consuming 212 dwellings and stores in the heart of the recently rebuilt town. The only edifice of importance which almost miraculously escaped the fury of the flames was the new church, although the town hall adjoining it was destroyed.

The church built by Don Andres Almonester was blessed December 23, 1794, and the Most Holy Sacrament transferred to it. It witnessed the ceremony of the exchange of flags on December 1, 1803, when the royal red and yellow emblem of Spain fluttered down the high flagstaff in the *Plaza de Armas* and the tricolor of Napoleon's France took its place for twenty short days, only to be succeeded by the banner of fifteen stars and fifteen stripes of the young United States.

In 1814 changes were made in the facade of the Cathedral and the two sides were crowned by low spires, following designs made by H. S. Boneval Latrobe, the son of Benjamin H. Latrobe. It appears that the younger Latrobe's plans also included the erection of a central spire and belfry, but this addition was not made until ten years later when a builder named Le Riche is said to have made this alteration.

When Don Andres' church was erected its parish was a part of the Diocese of Havana, but in 1793 Louisiana and the Floridas (East and West) were erected into a separate diocese and Don Luis de Penalver y Cardenas was appointed first bishop of Louisiana. When he arrived in New Orleans in July 1795 and took possession of the parish church, it became the *Catedral de San Luis* and has remained a cathedral ever since. At this time Padre Francisco Antonio Ildefonso Moreno y Arze, a Spanish Capuchin friar of Sedella, Granada, Spain, better remembered in New Orleans as Fray Antonio de Sedella, returned to New Orleans and was installed as *cura* or pastor of the Cathedral, a post he held until his death in 1829. Fray Antonio was a stormy petrel throughout his life in the old town and he not only clashed with his ecclesiastical authorities but even with the civil authorities, and his actions were investigated by American officials following the Louisiana Purchase.

At one time so serious were the difficulties between Padre Antonio and Father Patrick Walsh, who had been left in charge of the spiritual affairs of the diocese when Bishop Penalver was elevated and transferred to the Archepiscopal See of Guatemala, that Father Walsh withdrew the clergy from the Cathedral and designated the chapel of the Ursulines' Convent as the parish church. Father Antonio had himself elected pastor of his congregation and placed the Cathedral in the hands of a body of church wardens. There were several such clashes and it was not until Bishop Blanc took the matter of authority to the Supreme Court of Louisiana, and won that high court's decision, that the question was finally settled.

The architecture of the Cathedral is not now, nor has it ever been, what architects designate "pure," but it never has been wanting in effect. In 1849 the wardens of the Cathedral, headed by Dr. Isadore Labatut, decided that this old home of worship needed not only restoration but enlargement, and Jacques Nicolas B. de Pouilly, who had already won fame by his designs for the Saint Louis Hotel and other buildings in the Vieux Carré, was commissioned to draw up suitable plans. The first submitted called for an outlay of $77,000. Deciding this would be too costly, the architect made modified plans which cut down costs to $19,000, and the contractor, John Patrick Kirwan, agreed to finish the work in sixteen months. On the night of January 19, 1850, the central tower fell, wrecking not only the roof but smashing part of the walls. This accident raised the cost of reconditioning to a total of $30,000.

Architect de Pouilly's designs changing the appearance of the facade and the present portico, with its columns and pilasters, date from this year. Although the

Wrought-iron grillwork on the Cabildo

church originally erected by Almonester has been considerably altered, enlarged, and improved, it has never been *wholly rebuilt,* as has been claimed.

THE CABILDO

On either side of the Saint Louis Cathedral are two massive buildings which share with the place of worship historic importance. On the left, as we face this trio of architectural giants, is the *Cabildo,* the finest building erected for administrative purposes in the Louisiana province by the Spanish.

The name now given this building properly stands for the legislative assembly of the Spanish colonial government, the *Very Illustrious Cabildo,* and to call this building the "Cabildo" would be like calling our national capitol the "Congress." During the time the members of the Cabildo occupied the building it was termed by them *Casa Capitular* or "Capitol House."

When the French ruled for twenty days in 1803, this administration building was designated as *Maison de Ville* and, sometimes, *Hôtel de Ville* or, as we would say it, "Town Hall," and the French name persisted for many years after the Americans took over New Orleans.

The Spanish erected an administration building on this site in 1770 and from it ruled the province until the structure fell prey to the flames of the Good Friday fire of 1788. Another building set up on the foundations of the old was burned to the ground when the December fire of 1794 again swept the town.

In 1795 the members of the *Illustrious Cabildo* entered into a contract with Don Andres Almonester y Roxas, the same good Catholic who had erected the Saint Louis Cathedral as a present to the city, to build a new capitol house. Not having the necessary funds to pay for the construction of the new seat of government, Governor Baron de Carondelet solved this problem by borrowing the necessary money from the man who was to build the structure. Consequently, Don Andres

Cabildo, Cathedral, and Presbytere as they were in 1803 when New Orleans came into the possession of the United States, from an engraving by J. L. Boqueta de Woiseri

The nine semicircular arches of the Cabildo and Presbytere have long invited
the best efforts of artists, etchers, and photographers to picture them
(drawn and copyrighted by Morris Henry Hobbs)

The Cabildo gates (drawn by Joseph Pennell in 1882, copyrighted by *Century* magazine)

was not only its builder but its financial angel and architect as well, though he was assisted in its designing by Gilberto Guilleman, adjutant of the *Plaza.*

The *Very Illustrious Cabildo,* for whom this building was erected, was a deliberative body administering the affairs of New Orleans as would a commission council today, but it also had judicial powers. However, the building was more than a city hall in the days of Spanish rule. It was the seat of administration for the entire province of Louisiana for in it sat the law courts, both civil and criminal, as well as the sessions of the municipal corporation of *Nueva Orleans,* and was frequently referred to as the *"Principal."*

As originally built the Cabildo was a sturdy two-story structure holding close to the Spanish influence in architecture. The brick walls were stuccoed, the roof was flat and covered with flat tiles, with plaster ornaments or corbels regularly spaced to relieve the flatness of the top. The present mansard roof, added in 1847, serves but one purpose—to spoil the harmony of line. The pediment of the Cabildo, the triangular section just above the central entrance way, originally was embellished

The Cabildo as it appeared when originally built (drawn by Joseph Pennell, copyrighted by *Century* magazine)

with the Royal Arms of Spain, made by Le Prévost, a local sculptor, who charged sixty *pesos* for his wood carving. After the Louisiana Purchase the Spanish arms were removed and the American eagle, with the shield of the Union on its breast, replaced the insignia of Castile.

We learn from the records of the *Very Illustrious Cabildo* the cost of the building. In 1803, about the time word was received that Louisiana was to be returned to France, the *Cabildo* received an address from Don Gilberto Guilleman, adjutant of the *Plaza*, in which he claimed "as the *casas capitulares* were built in compliance of plans he had made, he requested an appraisement to satisfy his demands, with a discount of 500 *pesos* already received on account." His claim was referred to Almonester's widow. Three months later, when it became known that the Americans and not the French would be the new masters of Louisiana, Señora Luisa de la Ronde Almonester made her demand on the city's ruling body for the balance due her husband's estate for the construction of the *casas capitulares*. *Regidor* Don Juan de Castanedo advised his fellows that 27,500 *pesos* had already been paid the Almonester estate and 500 *pesos* paid Señor Guilleman, which left a balance due of exactly 4,348 *pesos* and six *reales*. The Cabildo members thereupon agreed to pay this balance "if any of the city tax funds were left." It seems that the city treasury was somewhat in the condition of Mother Hubbard's cupboard and Señora Almonester appealed to Governor Salcedo for what was due, and this indicated the building construction costs were 32,348 *pesos* and six *reales*.

In this very building took place in 1803 the transfer of Louisiana from Spain to France and, twenty days later, the transfer from France to the United States. The dignitaries of the three nations officially gave and received the province in the large room on the second floor now, as then, known as the *Sala Capitular*. The Cabildo now houses the historical and art sections of the Louisiana State Museum where is on display a remarkable and valuable exhibit of historical documents, portraits, mementos, furniture, costumes, and relics all having to do with Louisiana's colorful history. No visitor to New Orleans should neglect to inspect this most interesting museum.

THE PRESBYTERE

On the lower side of the Saint Louis Cathedral is the Presbytere, which resembles the Cabildo as one identical twin resembles another. Although given an ecclesiastical name, it is owned by the state of Louisiana and forms a part of the state museum.

Although usually stated to have been built in 1813, ten years after the Americans took possession of Louisiana, we now know, from documents of the Spanish period, that this structure had its foundations set even before those of the Cabildo were laid by Almonester's slaves. While it had not progressed beyond the first story when the Stars and Stripes first waved from the tall staff in the center of the *Place d'Armes*, its *rez-de-chaussée* had been completed and the arched columns were in place, as an old engraving of that time strikingly shows. In the *Cabildo* records is to be found a document which states that Don Andres Almonester is to build the "*Casa Capitular* upon the same plan as the *Casa Curial* is constructed, which occupies the other side of the Church, with the idea of making the *Plaza de Armas* uniform, which in fact would beautify it so that they will form two equal wings to the Temple." The Temple, in this case, means the Cathedral.

The *Casa Curial,* meaning a house for ecclesiastical purposes, quite similar to the meaning of the French term *presbytere,* which we now attach to the building, was probably begun in 1793, but Don Almonester had only finished the foundations

New Orleans as it was in 1803, from a map by J. L. Boqueta de Woiseri

and lower floor when the second disastrous fire of December 8, 1794, destroyed the buildings on the other side of the church and it was necessary for a new *Casa Capitular* to be built immediately. This necessity probably put a stop to building operations on the *Curial* and as it, together with the Cathedral, were to be gifts from Almonester, the benefactor's death ended all gratis building activities.

In the early days of the settlement of the city this site was occupied by a Capuchin monastery, whose garden extended back to *rue Royale,* so it was quite proper to have such a church house next to the place of worship. *Cabildo* documents prove that Almonester's widow brought suit to be absolved from being made to finish the construction of the *Curial* and when she lost the suit in the lower court she appealed to the *Audencia* in Havana and in 1813 won out in her contention. It was in that year, in all likelihood, that the American government completed the structure for at that time the state government placed some of its lower courts, courts of appeals, and the supreme court in the building. In March 1831, Denis Prieur, then mayor, gave the wardens of the Cathedral $10,500 for the land in the rear of the Presbytere, a plot 40 x 122 feet, for the purpose of constructing *"ruelle d'Orléans Nord,"* and it was at this same time that the Cathedral Garden was established.

Twenty-two years later, May 17, 1853, Mayor A. D. Crossman paid the wardens of the Saint Louis Cathedral $55,000 for the Presbytere. In the act of sale it was claimed that the church had remained in continuous possession of the property since 1745 when it had been given a grant by Le Normant, the intendant, and Vaudreuil, the governor. Although the city had been in possession of the building and its lower courts had dispensed justice in its rooms for more than forty years, it is likewise true that the city and state recognized church ownership in 1847, when the mansard roof was placed on the Cabildo, for the same plans were submitted to the church wardens for a like addition to the Presbytere, costs to be borne by the church society.

The fronts of the two buildings are similar. The lower story is of the Tuscan order, with a wide portico along the facade supported by ten columns between nine semicircular arches. The four arches in the center are supported in front by Tuscan columns and those at the angles by two clustered pilasters.

MADAME PONTALBA'S BUILDINGS

The two block-long red-brick buildings fronting either side of Jackson Square, looking for all the world like two companies of red-uniformed soldiers drawn up stiffly on parade, are the Pontalba apartments, said to be the first of their kind erected. They take their title from the married name of the daughter of Don Andres Almonester y Roxas, the wealthy Spaniard who built the Cathedral, Cabildo, and Presbytere.

When Almonester came to Louisiana in the train of Don Alessandro O'Reilly he was a widower and a lowly *escribano* or notary. In twenty years he accumulated a fortune. In 1778 he acquired two plots of ground facing the *Place d'Armes*, one in

Cast-iron balcony on the Pontalba Building

St. Ann and the other in St. Peter Street, each running from the river to Chartres. From the settling of the city these two sites had been government property and by what right Don Pedro Moris could sell these choice parcels to Almonester is not now clear. At any rate on November 13, 1778, Almonester became the owner.

It was not until he was sixty-two that he decide upon a second marriage. His choice was Louise de la Ronde, who was twenty-nine, well past the usual marrying age of beautiful, well-to-do Louisiana maids. From this union were born two daughters—only the younger surviving infancy. She was Micaëla Leonarda Antonia Almonester y Roxas y Broutin, born November 6, 1795, when her father was seventy-one years old. She was only two and one-half years old when Don Andres died. She was almost sixteen when she married her cousin, Joseph Xavier Celestin Delfau de Pontalba, who was only twenty, a dispensation being procured from Rome for the degree of consanguinity existing between the two. It proved to be the most famous of all marriages in New Orleans and was performed by Fray Antonio de Sedella on October 23, 1811.

Micaëla became the mother of three sons but the marriage between the representatives of the two richest families in Louisiana did not prove to be a happy one. Her husband's father, Baron Joseph Xavier de Pontalba, angered at the separation and the refusal of his daughter-in-law to give up control of her fortune, made threats against her and ordered her away from his *Château Mont l'Evêque* in France. Micaëla, however, did go to the Château to see her husband on matters concerning the actions of their eldest son. While she was alone in her room, the Baron, her father-in-law, entered with a pistol in each hand. After a few words he shot her and, after going to his own room, shot himself in the head.

Micaëla's wounds were many and dangerous, but she recovered. Her husband, because of his father's death, had become a baron but Micaëla never held the title of baroness, even a short time, because the divorce followed almost immediately.

The French revolution of 1848 caused Micaëla to leave Paris and to return to her native city. It was then that she took steps to improve and beautify the historic

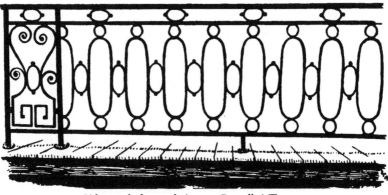

Side panel of wrought iron on Pontalba's Taverne

Place d'Armes, the name of which, at her insistence, was changed to Jackson Square. She contributed generously toward the movement to erect the equestrian statue of Old Hickory, today the dominating feature of that open spot in the heart of the Vieux Carré.

At the same time she planned the erection of the two rows of houses that flank the square on St. Peter and St. Ann streets. The plans were drawn by James Gallier the elder and the contract for the sixteen buildings on the St. Peter street side was given to Samuel Stewart, July 20, 1849, the contractor agreeing to erect them for $156,000. Work began at once and the day before Christmas, 1849, the same contractor agreed to put up the St. Ann street building for $146,000. The apartments on the St. Peter street side were to be finished and ready for occupancy May 1, 1850, and the buildings on the lower side of the square to be completed by the first of November of the same year.

It was not until the first of March, 1851, that Madame de Pontalba, as she insisted she should be addressed, signed rental leases. At that time the drift of business was away from the old section of town and she hoped her new combination apartment houses and business shops would cause business to return to the Vieux Carré. It proved a vain hope.

After the buildings were completed Madame de Pontalba, and her sons Alfred and Gaston, lived in the building at No. 5 (now 508) St. Peter Street, and that was the place occupied by Jenny Lind, the Swedish Nightingale, when that singer visited New Orleans.

One of the favorite traditions of New Orleans links the name of Micaëla with that of John McDonogh, the tight-fisted Scot who came to New Orleans from Baltimore to make his fortune. The tradition claims he aspired to the hand of Almonester's daughter and . . . but let us read the tradition as it is copied and recopied in some guide leaflets:

> *The history of John McDonogh reads like a romance in these latter days. In 1800 he came to New Orleans where he went into business on his own account, and was soon regarded as one of the most successful and wealthy of men. In 1806, young, gay, and*

dashing and a general favorite, not only in business circles but in the most exclusive homes of the old Creole noblesse, he retired from commercial life and devoted himself to the management of his large estates. He opened a magnificent home, kept a numerous retinue of slaves, fine horses and equipage, and was considered one of the most desirable matches in the French Quarter. But young McDonogh aspired high, and none pleased him so well as the beautiful daughter of Don Almonester, the Spanish colonial philanthropist and magnate of New Orleans. The proud nobleman rejected the suit, declaring that a daughter of his noble race should never ally herself to a plebeian. Stung to the heart, McDonogh withdrew and his grief and mortification weighed so heavily upon him that he swore he would have more money than all the Almonesters and Pontalbas put together, and that his name would live when their proud titles would have sunk into oblivion.

The main faults in this touching tradition are: Almonester had been in his grave two years when McDonogh came to New Orleans and in 1806, when McDonogh supposedly aspired to Micaëla's hand, she was only nine years old and being taught by the nuns of the Ursulines' Convent. However such anachronisms do not seem to abash the historians on the sight-seeing buses.

The Pontalba buildings are now state and city owned. Those in St. Peter Street were purchased by the city government, and the St. Ann Street apartments were acquired by William Ratcliffe Irby and given to the Louisiana State Museum. When they were finished in 1851 they aroused the admiration of the citizens, and today, even in their tarnished beauty, they are most interesting to look upon. Visitors admire the series of spacious verandas embroidered with an elegance of tendril-like cast-iron work made in France, which displays, in frequent repetition, the intertwined *A P*—initials of the ill-fated union of the houses of Almonester and Pontalba.

PONTALBA'S *TAVERNE*   600 St. Peter St.

The old Moresque building at the southwest corner of Chartres and St. Peter streets, having on its balcony, which faces both streets, one of the finest examples of wrought-iron work to be found in New Orleans, was a famous inn for many

Wrought-iron corner design at Chartres and St. Peter streets

years after its erection. It is now a part of the Little Theatre and has long been a
subject of speculation as to its age, the identity of its builder, and its former usage.

It is usually pointed out as *Le Veau-qui-Tête*, "The Suckling Calf," a *taverne* noted
for its splendid cooking and the quality of the wines and other liquids served by its
jolly host. We learn from one of the earliest city directories, however, that "The
Suckling Calf" was not located at this corner but was in fact at old 58 *rue de la Levée*
(now 919 Decatur Street) and operated by R. Ravel, who not only conducted a hotel
there but also had well-patronized public baths.

A search of ancient notarial records proves that this building was erected in 1800
by Joseph Xavier de Pontalba (who, going to France, was made a baron by Napoleon) soon after he acquired the corner site and adjoining properties through
John Garnier, his agent. These purchases were made in joint ownership with Mme
Marie Céleste Elénore Macarty, widow of Don Esteban Miro, the Spanish governor of Louisiana from 1785 to 1791. This probably gave rise to the erroneous tradition that Spanish governors lived here.

Adjoining Pontalba's Inn are three other old-timers, each erected soon after the
second great New Orleans fire of 1794, and as we proceed up Chartres on our
sight-seeing tour we can examine them in turn.

627 CHARTRES STREET—Don José Fouque erected this brick building soon
after he purchased the site from Joseph X. Pontalba on February 4, 1795. This section had been swept clean by the fire of the preceding December and Governor El
Baron de Carondelet had issued an order that no more wooden structures could
be erected in this part of town. In 1809 Bradford & Anderson, printers, who published a newspaper and made things most miserable for Governor Claiborne, occupied the building.

625 CHARTRES STREET—The building adjoining, not quite as ancient, was evidently built by Joseph Cheyron in 1802, shortly after he had paid Pontalba *cuarto
mil quinientos* (4,500) *pesos* for the site.

BOSQUE'S HOME   617 CHARTRES ST.

We can and should be interested in this fine old mansion because of its antiquity,
but probably its most distinctive feature is the wrought-iron balcony railing. It is
not only a splendid example of the blacksmith's art but it carries in its center what
is probably the most unique monogram to be found in the Vieux Carré. The *B B*
differs from the other monograms we have seen, in that it is *backwards* when read
from the street. The initials are those of the building's constructor, Bartolome
Bosque, a prosperous merchant of the city in the good old Spanish days who built
it in 1795 after purchasing the site from Joseph X. Pontalba. Like many another
hidalgo of importance, Señor Bosque insisted that his initials should proclaim his
residence, so when the balcony railings were hammered out of wrought iron by
some skillful artisan of southern Spain and shipped across the Atlantic from
Cadiz, the monogram of the proud owner was a prominent part of the design.
Whether they were, in 1795, placed on the balcony in reverse is purely problemati-

Spanish wrought-iron balcony railing at 617 Chartres St.

cal—the probabilities being that this is the result of careless work of later repair-men who have replaced the railing wrong-side-to in the belief that such initials should be read by the inmates of the house and not by passers-by.

The Bartolome Bosque home has more historic interest than that of a reversed monogram—unique as it is. Here was born Suzette Bosque, who became the third wife of Governor Claiborne. After his death his widow, Suzette, known as "the most beautiful, fascinating, and coquettish woman in New Orleans," married John Randolph Grymes, an erratic but brilliant and noted attorney, one of numerous legal lights who was kept busy in the days before the Battle of New Orleans, repre-senting in court and keeping out of jail the celebrated Laffite brothers.

PERRILLIAT'S INN   624 CHARTRES ST.

Opposite Bartolome Bosque's old mansion at the corner of Chartres and Wilkin-son streets, and immediately adjoining the rear of Madame de Pontalba's St. Peter Street buildings, is a square, two-story structure once called the Cabildo Restau-rant. During the peaceful days following the Battle of New Orleans this corner inn, celebrated for its coffee, its wines, and billiard tables, was a popular gathering place for menfolk. Here they could exchange the latest bit of gossip or discuss poli-tics and Napoleon's incarceration and his probable future.

The building dates from 1816, the year the state government, which owned the property between the boundary now marked by the rear of the Pontalba buildings facing St. Peter Street, Decatur, Toulouse, and Chartres, cut through a short nar-row thoroughfare and named it Jefferson Street in honor of the president who had purchased Louisiana from France. The state house, which was then at the corner of Old Levée and Toulouse, and had been there since its erection by the French in 1761, was allowed a suitable garden space but the rest of the square was divided into building lots and leased to highest bidders for a term of twenty-five years.

"THE COURTYARD OF THE TWISTED VINE"   614 CHARTRES ST.

Had you happened to have been in old New Orleans in the early spring several decades ago, when plant life in courtyard and patio was bursting into a riot of bloom, and visited "The Courtyard of the Twisted Vine," you would have beheld one of the most beautiful floral sights imaginable.

The casual passerby in Chartres Street in the month of March might have strolled past the narrow passageway at 614 and never suspected that in the rear court was a mammoth wistaria vine which had transformed the gray courtyard into a place of purple loveliness—just as though the patio had put on its very best gown for Easter Sunday. But that sight is denied the visitor today for, when the old building was restored, it became necessary to prune severely the wistaria.

When the vine was at the height of its loveliness, various estimates were made as to its age. Research proves that it was planted in 1860 by Lena Schalck, whose father, Jacob Schalck, then owned this old but characteristic Chartres Street combination business and dwelling place, which made the vine eighty-four years old in the spring of 1944.

This house, and the one adjoining it at the corner, was built soon after Joseph Chardon leased the site from the state in 1816. The two buildings happily escaped the fire that consumed the old state house at Toulouse and Decatur streets in 1828. In 1844, when the state treasurer sold these properties, John McDonogh became the owner of "The Courtyard of the Twisted Vine" but it is doubtful that he ever lived here.

REYNES MANSION   601 CHARTRES ST.

At the northwest corner of Chartres and Toulouse streets is a building once occupied by Victor's Cafe whose age dates back to 1796, when Joseph Reynes purchased the site by exchanging a plantation tract on the Mississippi River (with a slave named John Henry thrown in for *lagniappe*) for the corner property. Madame Louise Briot, widow of François Caisergus, made the exchange. Reynes, who was a well-to-do merchant, retained possession until 1830, when he sold the mansion to François Gautier de Boismagny for $20,000. Although this structure has been pointed out as the one-time "palatial residence" of John McDonogh, the chain of realty transactions fails to show he ever owned, much less occupied it.

SITE OF FIRST FIRE   538 CHARTRES ST.

Diagonally across from the old Reynes mansion, or *deux encoignures*, as the French-speaking folk of the old city would have expressed it (or should we say, as do the little boys of the street, "cat-a-corner"), is the site on which stood the *casa* of Don José Vicente Nuñez, military treasurer of the province, a good Catholic who believed in observing every feast of the church. At 1:30 in the afternoon of March 21, 1788, the Good Friday of that year, while candles were burning before a shrine, a gust of wind blew the window curtains against the lighted tapers. A few moments later the entire house was ablaze. "The fire started with such fury, due to the strong south wind, it was impossible to control until four hours later," says the entry in the Cabildo records, "during which time four-fifths of the populated section of the city was reduced to ashes, including the parish church and house, the *Casa Capitular,* and city jail."

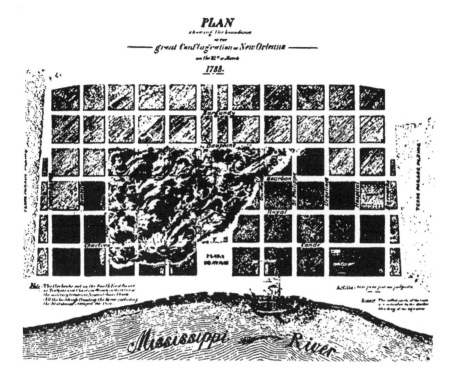

When the fire had spent its fury 856 houses, practically every dwelling place occupied by its leading citizens, had been consumed. All that escaped were the buildings along the levee in front of the Mississippi River, and one that was saved was the *Casa del Gobierno*, whose garden fronted the Nuñez home. It is worthy of comment that the city's second great fire happened on December 8, 1794, when the Feast of the Immaculate Conception was being celebrated. The present structure was built about 1830 by Major Louis Gally.

PHARMACIE DUFILHO   514 CHARTRES ST.

New Orleans, so the visitor will find when he explores the Vieux Carré, has two "Napoleon Houses." One is the fine old edifice, imposing in its lines in spite of the heavy hand that decay has laid upon it, at 514 Chartres Street, which once displayed a sign proclaiming it the "real" Napoleon House.

This once-upon-a-time stylish residence and business place was built by Louis Joseph Dufilho, Jr., a popular druggist of the old city who conducted his first pharmacy on Toulouse Street. On June 2, 1822, so we learn from a notarial act, Dufilho purchased from Philip Sadtler *"un emplacement situé rue Chartres entre les rues St. Louis et Toulouse."* It is quite likely that the construction was begun very soon after the purchase of the lot, for in 1823 the *Pharmacie* Dufilho was opened on the ground floor and the apothecary's family domiciled in the apartments above.

NAPOLEON HOUSE
OLD NEW ORLEANS

© M.H.HOBBS

Mayor Girod's mansion, also known as the "Napoleon House" from the tradition that it would be his home if he escaped from St. Helena and came to New Orleans

That this house could not have been built as a "refuge" for Napoleon is evidenced by the fact that the first news of the death of the Little Corporal was printed in the newsprints of New Orleans on September 10, 1821, and on Wednesday, December 19, a funeral service and mass were held in the Saint Louis Cathedral when, for the first and only time, an oration was delivered in this place of worship by a layman. The procession that passed through the streets formed in front of the Masonic Lodge of Charity and drew the black-draped catafalque to the Cathedral, where Judge Placide Canonge, a prominent Mason, delivered the oration.

It was six months after this public demonstration and nearly a year after Napoleon's death at St. Helena that apothecary Dufilho purchased the lot in Chartres Street on which he erected his popular drugstore, which continued in operation long after the apothecary's death. In 1855 it was sold to Dr. Joseph Dupas for $18,000, who leased the drugstore to J. Gourdon & Co., but in 1859 Dr. Dupas took over the business, prescribed for his patients, and then filled his own prescriptions!

The City of New Orleans, in conjunction with Loyola University, has converted this old structure into a museum housing an old-time pharmacy.

"THE NAPOLEON HOUSE"   500 CHARTRES ST.

This imposing edifice, typical of the Spanish-Creole architecture of old New Orleans, is known to most Orleanians and all visitors as "The Napoleon House." It gained this name from a tradition that while the former emperor of the French and *ci-devant* "Master of the World" was a prisoner of the British on the island of St. Helena, a group of his admirers in New Orleans, headed by Mayor Nicolas Girod, planned his rescue and proposed to give him domicile in the territory he had sold to the United States for four cents an acre.

Mayor Girod's plan, according to the tradition that defies substantiation, planned to engage the services of a stalwart crew of jolly rogers, on a swift sailing vessel to be commanded by a pirate, which was to sail secretly to the island prison, surprise and overpower the guards, rescue Napoleon, and transport him to New Orleans. To house suitably the man who lost everything at Waterloo, Mayor Girod agreed to build a mansion for Bonaparte—and this is the very mansion.

The scheme found many backers, according to tradition, and the expedition was to be commanded by Captain St. Ange Bossière, "whose yacht was a long, low, black, raking schooner named *Seraphine*." As might be suspected, this rescue tale grew and was told with variations, and pirates, such as Dominique You, René Béluche, and other members of Jean Laffite's jolly Baratarian band, displaced Captain Bossière in the telling. Whether with Bossière, Béluche, or You as commander, plans were at last completed and, believe it or not, the very day that the *Seraphine* was ready to drop down the river and make out over the bounding main in the direction of St. Helena, came the word to New Orleans that Napoleon had died!

A variation of this venerable tradition, and the one believed by Judge Castellanos to be the correct version, is as follows. When Napoleon escaped from Elba in 1815, the news reached New Orleans at a time the leading citizens were witnessing a performance in the St. Philip Street theatre. Wildest enthusiasm greeted this announcement, made from the stage, and the entire audience filed from the theatre and gathered with the rest of the excited population at the Cabildo. The impression then was that Napoleon would desert France and seek refuge in America and that, in all probability, New Orleans would be his port of entry. Nicolas Girod, the city's mayor at that time, is said to have made a speech in which he promised, if Bonaparte would come to New Orleans, he would place his own residence at the disposal of the illustrious exile.

The so-called Napoleon House, which will be readily identified by the belvedere atop its roof, was owned for many years by Mayor Girod. Notarial records prove that on September 4, 1798, this *casa* was only two stories high when it was sold by the heirs of Doña Angela Monget to Don Claudio Francisco Girod, a wealthy planter of the Lafourche country. In this act the *casa* is described: "*Une maison à étage composée au rez-de-chaussée d'un magasin, trois chambres à feu au-dessus et un magasin, la dite maison couverte en tuiles et batie en briques, plus dans la cour deux cuisines et deux chambres au-dessus un petit magasin.*"

In 1814 Claude François Girod died and this property passed to his brother Nicolas, then serving his first term as the first elected mayor of the city, and the place remained under his ownership until his death in 1841. The year when the third story was added and the belvedere placed on the roof has not been established.

CHESNEAU MANSION   533 ST. LOUIS ST.

Let us turn into St. Louis Street in the direction of the river for a moment to inspect the building that adjoins Nicolas Girod's home. It, too, is a fine old building, a relic of the days of the Spanish builders. Unfortunately the structure has become known in late years as the "Lafitte Bank." As a matter of fact, there was never a bank of that name in New Orleans and this building was never put to such a use.

Architects have long admired the building's simple beauty and sturdy construction and various estimates have been made as to its exact age. It was erected by Jean Louis Chesneau, quite probably just after he secured the site from the widow of Jean Turpin for 4,015 *pesos* on October 6, 1800. In 1860, the house of Lafitte & Dufilho, "commission merchants and real estate," moved into old 19 St. Louis Street, and remained there until the firm was liquidated in 1886. It was never a bank and Charles Lafitte, the commission merchant, was not related to the Lafites, the famous Baratarian smuggling brothers, as can be determined by the spelling of the family name.

MASPERO'S EXCHANGE   440 CHARTRES ST.

Probably no other building in the Vieux Carré is more deserving of historical veneration than this square two-story plastered-brick edifice on the southeast corner of Chartres and St. Louis streets, directly *vis-à-vis* the big Nicolas Girod building. Our veneration can be in acknowledgment of the many years it has stood on this very spot, or it can be for the many stirring events that have transpired within its stout walls since that day in June 1788 when Don Juan Paillet purchased the lots from Don Narciso Alva and on the ruins of Señor Alva's *casa*, which had been burned to the ground during the Good Friday fire of that year, built the structure that has become not only a tradition but a reality in the history of the city.

Although Juan Paillet built this house and the quaint narrow one adjoining it in Chartres Street, and the two buildings continued in the possession of his family until 1878, the main building on the corner is best known by the name of one of its tenants—Pierre Maspero, who here carried on a coffeehouse and exchange called *La Bourse de Maspero,* or as the Americans called it, "Maspero's Exchange."

It was in the closing days of 1814 that this old home of Señor Paillet won its historic fame. Then it was that a red-coated army was planning to capture the old city. A fighting man was hastening to the city but before Andrew Jackson arrived the citizens of New Orleans had formed a Committee of Public Safety and its members selected Maspero's Exchange as headquarters. It was the appeal of this committee that had welded the citizens of the city into one fighting unit when General Jackson arrived to command.

D'ESTREHAN RESIDENCE   400 CHARTRES ST.

Although this ancient brick pile at the northeast corner of Chartres and Conti streets, bearing the number 400, carried in its fine wrought-iron balcony railing the monogram *F M P,* it was originally the home of Jean Noël d'Estrehan (as the well-known Louisiana name of Destrehan was originally spelled) and it was only after that gentleman's death in 1823 that the mansion, built of Holland bricks, passed to another owner.

Ancient documents show that d'Estrehan purchased the site from Pierre Duclide Barran on March 12, 1802, and it is quite probable that the town house was erected just before those twenty momentous days in 1803 when Louisiana was retroceded to France by Spain, and then by France to the infant United States.

It was not until 1825 that Mme Céleste Robin de Logny, Noël's widow, sold the residence to François Marie Perrilliat for $24,000. It is quite evident that the new owner, in improving the place, as was the style in those days, had his initials forged in the corner balcony. It is one of the most graceful monograms found in the Vieux Carré.

U.S. BRANCH BANK   301 CHARTRES ST.

When the Americans came into possession of Louisiana and New Orleans in 1803, there was not a bank in the province or city. In 1805 Governor Claiborne authorized the organization of the Bank of Louisiana, which was established at 417 Royal Street, and in the same year the U.S. Bank of Philadelphia decided to open a branch in New Orleans. In April 1805, it bought this site.

The U.S. Branch Bank, designated then as *Banque des Etats-Unis, ou Bureau d'Escompte et de Dépôt*, set up in business and remained here until 1813 when the building and grounds were sold to Honoré Landreaux. Whether this is the identical building used by the old bank is not known; notarial records throw no light on this moot question.

It was on this site that the Ursuline nuns were domiciled from the date of their arrival in 1727, to the time their first convent was built and thrown open for occupancy in 1734. During the intervening seven years they taught the colonist's daughters in a habitation owned by W. Knolly, known as the Ste. Reine Concession.

Arrows form the strings of the lyre on this balcony railing at 917 Toulouse St.

Down Bourbon Street

OUR FIRST SIGHT-SEEING round trip in the Vieux Carré is finished when we again reach Canal Street. There are, however, many other places of interest in the Old Square we did not see in our promenade along *rue Royale* or in the busy commercial street that was named in honor of the *duc du Chartres*, nor did short excursions into side streets exhaust all there is worth seeing in what was the original limits of old New Orleans.

We should not fail to visit the old French Market and on our way there note a few of the architectural landmarks still defying time and decay in what was *rue de la Levée* before it was renamed for Stephen Decatur.

Away from the river are three ancient streets, Bourbon, Dauphine, and Burgundy, and in each, as well as in the cross streets near them, are the old homes of the aristocratic Creoles of yesteryear, with their enticing courtyards, arched pillars, domed corridors, fan-shaped transoms, and monogramed wrought- and cast-iron balcony grilles.

We can start the Bourbon Street promenade exactly as we made our pilgrimage in old Royal Street, by starting where Bourbon has its beginning at Canal Street. Although the first few blocks may be devoid of mementos of a historical past, we will soon arrive in a section of the original city where history was made in days that are gone forever.

GALATOIRE'S   209 BOURBON ST.

While it is claimed that the only rival to New Orleans in the art of preparing food for the table is the city of Paris, certain gourmets, those who have literally eaten their way around the world, vehemently declare that the talented chefs of the Crescent City are superior in many ways to those of *La Belle France* . . . that at Antoine's, *La Louisiane*, Galatoire's, Arnaud's, and Broussard's, viands are prepared so as to merit the name of Art in cookery.

Galatoire's has long been an institution in the Vieux Carré. The present restaurant was established by Jean Galatoire in 1905, who took over a restaurant that had been occupying this same building under the name of Victor's, which had been

This narrow passageway, between the Cabildo and the Cathedral, is officially ruelle
d'Orléans sud, *but most people like to believe pirates used it exclusively*
(drawn and copyrighted by Morris Henry Hobbs)

established a quarter of a century before by Victor Béro. The building was erected in 1831, and the ironwork on the two balconies is notable for the lyres in the center of each railing.

OLD ABSINTHE HOUSE   238 BOURBON ST.

Of all the ancient buildings of the Vieux Carré none has been pictured more, none has had more fantastic tales told about it, than has the old square plastered-brick building at the southeast corner of Bourbon and Bienville streets. It gained its name "The Old Absinthe House" from the fact that for the past century this potent green drink made from wormwood was dispensed from the old bar that long was a distinctive feature of the ancient structure. The bar, its square of marble having a surface pitted by the water drippings from the faucet, was removed during the dreary days of the prohibition experiment and has found its way to another liquid-dispensing establishment which now flaunts an advertisement that there is to be found "the original Absinthe House *bar.*"

When this structure was erected by Pedro Font and Francisco Juncadella, soon after Juncadella purchased the corner site from Dame Marie Car on March 23, 1806, it was not a coffee shop but the combination residence and food establishment of Font & Juncadella, importers of foodstuffs, wines, and other goods from their native city of Barcelona, Spain. Their first commission house had been established at Bourbon and St. Ann in 1802 but an increasing business demanded a more desirable location and the present building was constructed.

The combination mansion and commission establishment built by Francisco Juncadella in 1806 was owned by his and Pedro Font's descendants well into the twentieth century. Juncadella was a native of Catalonge, Spain, who two weeks before he died on August 13, 1820, made his will and, after commending his soul to his maker and specifying the number of candles he wanted burned, bequeathed his worldly goods to his wife, also a native of Barcelona. His desire was that his partner, Pedro Font, to whom he was related by marriage, should carry on the prosperous business they had built up in old New Orleans.

Doña Rosa Juncadella returned to her native Barcelona with her two small daughters and in 1828 married Dr. Don José Cusachs, by whom she had two sons. She died in 1857, her eldest daughter Françoise died without being married, and Emerée Mercedes, who married Domingo de Caralt, was also without issue when she passed away in 1893.

When the Widow Juncadella and Pedro Font returned to Spain, their properties were left in the hands of her relatives, Jacinto, Leopold, and P. O. Aleix. In 1838 this structure was a shoe shop, in 1843 a grocery store, and in 1861 Jacinto and P. O. Aleix converted the Juncadella mansion for the first time into a coffeehouse. In 1870 they employed Cayetano Ferrér, a Catalàn from Barcelona, as chief bartender. This skilled drink-mixer had come to New Orleans several years before and won instant recognition from the discriminating bibbers of the town for the way he mixed and served palatable concoctions in the basement bar of the old French Opera House. In 1874 Cayetano Ferrér took over the lease of the old Juncadella

Old Absinthe House, probably the best known of all the old buildings in old New Orleans, erected in 1806, is at Bourbon and Bienville streets (drawn and copyrighted by Morris Henry Hobbs)

mansion and for the first time it was listed and known as the "Absinthe Room." Drip, drip, drip, drip—water fell from the fountain faucet into the green liquid, all was frappéd, and the fame of this specialty spread far beyond the limits of the Crescent City.

The entire Ferrér family, father, mother, Uncle Leon, and the three sons, Felix, Paul, and Jacinto, continued to serve delighted customers in what became, in 1886, "The Old Absinthe Room." When Cayetano Ferrér passed on to his reward in 1889, his widow and sons carried on the café business and the secret of serving an absinthe frappé that no other refreshment parlor in New Orleans could success-fully duplicate. It was not until 1890, however, that the mansion built by Francisco Juncadella in 1806 was first called by the distinctive name it bears today—"The Old Absinthe House."

ARNAUD'S   811 BIENVILLE ST.

Cooking in New Orleans has a cachet all its own; "*C'est la cuisine Créole.*" Although the delicacy and artistry of the French school predominates through it, it has also the piquancy and tang of the Spanish, with the simplicity and wholesomeness so favored by the early settlers and builders. The restaurant originated by Arnaud Cazenave, and baptized, as is the custom, with his given name, is one of the favored shrines of those who find that while New Orleans is Second Port, U.S.A., it is sec-ond to no other city in the variety and excellence of its food. Arnaud's occupies buildings constructed February 27, 1833, by Victor Seghers.

JUNCADELLA'S *EPICERIE*   301 BOURBON ST.

Diagonally opposite the Old Absinthe House is a low, squat, one-story plastered-brick building. Years ago it was an *épicerie,* or grocery, owned and operated by Pedro Font and Francisco Juncadella. Pedro Font, whose wife was Doña Francisca Pasant y Juncadella, retired to his native Spain to enjoy the fruits of his fortune making in New Orleans, and was sixty-three when he died in Barcelona in 1828. The old grocery shop, which later became a shoe and boot store, was probably built during the Spanish domination although its exact date of erection has not been located.

305 BOURBON STREET—Immediately adjoining the old Juncadella-Font gro-cery, this building was built in 1819 by Dame Marguerite Clark, the widow of Claude Chabot, soon after she purchased the site.

JUDAH P. BENJAMIN'S   327 BOURBON ST.

The bow and arrow design of the cast iron which guards the balcony of the three-story mansion at 327 Bourbon Street is not the only feature about this house that deserves our attention. It was here that Judah Philip Benjamin, noted Jewish Louisiana lawyer and statesman, wooed and won the hand of Natalie St. Martin and here lived with the bride's parents.

Benjamin, born a British subject at St. Thomas in the West Indies, had a distin-guished if varied career. He was educated at Yale, entered a lawyer's office in New

Orleans, with John Slidell compiled a digest of the laws of Louisiana, and became a United States senator. In 1861 he withdrew from the Senate, espoused the cause of the states that sought to secede, was appointed the attorney-general, and became "the brains of the Confederacy." During the last two years of the war he was secretary of state. When the Confederacy failed, Benjamin fled to Florida, went to sea in an open boat and, after many vicissitudes, reached England as an exile. In a few years he attained prominence at the British bar and was seriously considered for elevation to the bench. He died in Paris in 1884, was baptized, by orders of his wife, in the Catholic faith, and was so buried.

The mansion was built by Auguste St. Martin in 1835 and here he lived with his wife and two children, Jules, his son, and Natalie, his daughter who married Judah P. Benjamin.

339 BOURBON STREET—The one-story structure at the corner of Bourbon and Conti streets occupies an old structure that was erected by Don André Guillory some years prior to 1826, when he sold it to François Boisdoré.

BROUSSARD'S RESTAURANT   819 CONTI ST.

As we continue our promenade down Bourbon Street, we can glance to the left as we pass Conti Street to note at 819 the buildings that house another distinctive restaurant of the Vieux Carré—Broussard's. The buildings that it occupies are not old but they do occupy the site of a famous institution of learning, Jefferson Academy. Broussard's cuisine lives up to the traditions and high standards set by Creole cookery.

400 BOURBON STREET—Proudly advertising the fact that within is to be found the "Old Absinthe House Bar" is a thirst-quenching establishment that has, indeed, the very bar that once was a feature of the original "Old Absinthe House," a block away. These three-story buildings were erected in 1838 by Randall Curell, a wealthy merchant.

HERMANN-GRIMA HISTORIC HOUSE   820 ST. LOUIS ST.

In the one-time fashionable street, christened with a saintly and kingly name, a few steps off Bourbon we find a truly aristocratic-looking home, one that stands out from other mansions in the Old Square by the very apparent fact that it resembles more the red brick colonial homes of New England than it does the characteristic Hispano-Creole style of architecture which predominates in old New Orleans. For many years it was known as the "Grima House" despite the fact that Felix Grima, a noted attorney and notary, who had owned it for many years, did not build it.

While it has not been definitely ascertained just when it was erected, or what architect designed it, the probabilities are that Samuel Hermann, Sr., a wealthy commission merchant, had it erected soon after he purchased the site, on May 19, 1823. The mansion remained the home of the Hermanns until 1844 when, owing to financial difficulties, Samuel Hermann and his son were forced to realize upon all their properties. It was then that Felix Grima purchased the mansion, and it remained the Grima home through the rigors of the Civil War. The architecture of the old Grima home has much about it to be admired, within as well as without. The house has been restored by the Christian Woman's Exchange and is open to the public for tours.

826 ST. LOUIS STREET—To designate the residence immediately adjoining the old Grima home as "the house that Jacques built" is only to pay tribute to one of the most talented architects who designed so many of the more noteworthy buildings now standing in the Vieux Carré. He was Jacques N. B. de Pouilly, the same who first visualized on paper and then built the original Saint Louis Hotel, who reconstructed the Saint Louis Cathedral, and designed the Union Bank in Royal Street, to mention only three of his architectural triumphs.

On March 17, 1842, Edouard Bertus, who had made his money by being one of the best dancing masters of the city, contracted with architect de Pouilly and his partner, Ernest Goudchaux, to build, at a cost of $11,120, the residence at 826 St. Louis Street. The original plans are still preserved in the old notarial act that bound the *entrepreneurs* to a faithful performance of their duties and they contain the carefully executed pen-and-ink drawings of de Pouilly which prove him a talented artist as well as designer.

LAFCADIO HEARN'S ROOMS   516 BOURBON ST.

Upon our return to Bourbon Street to take up our interrupted stroll down this ancient thoroughfare we will see in this block a number of old structures that have little of historic interest, although some were built so long ago that they deserve attention from this fact alone.

The house at 516 Bourbon holds particular interest to writers and readers of exquisite English because there Lafcadio Hearn struggled on alone in a humble inexpensive rented room soon after he came to New Orleans in 1878. It was from this house that the half-blind little writer, dressed in cheap and clumsy clothes, erratic and often dependent on charity, wandered forth to experience the charm of the Vieux Carré—its old buildings and artistic nooks, its warm indolence, its street chatter and *patios,* the quaint customs of blacks and whites—and became an ardent worshipper of this ancient seat of Louisiana Creole culture.

His special genius found vent in his writings . . . "so exotic and bizarre in content, so gleaming and richly colored, so painstakingly set to paper," Allen Nevins tells us. "He enameled and polished each paragraph with meticulous care. Over each essay the near-sighted word-jeweler toiled like a lapidary over his precious gems."

The house in which Lafcadio Hearn lodged when he was employed on the old *City Item* was built for Jean Baptiste Modeste Lefebre by Ducayet & Dumingon soon after he purchased the site on March 28, 1827.

513-515 BOURBON STREET—The one-story building opposite Lefebre's mansion is an old-timer too. It was built in 1816 by Jean Lacoste.

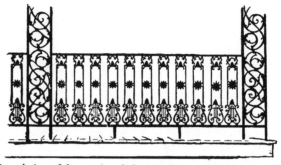

Lyre design of the cast-iron balcony railing at 532 Bourbon St.

ROUZAN RESIDENCE   522 BOURBON ST.

Opposite the site of the old French Opera House is a once-fine edifice that has departed from its former grandeur but, even in its dog days, it is interesting and compelling. Up to 1884 it was the town residence of Jacques Philippe Meffre Rouzan, a wealthy planter of East Baton Rouge Parish, who built it soon after he purchased the site in 1838 from the estate of Marc Lafitte, the old-time notary.

The old residence has many attractive features, a spacious courtyard, and a number of solid outbuildings. Only when the former Rouzan residence is observed from a distance can the tower or belvedere atop the roof be noted.

532 BOURBON STREET—This building with the decorative balcony railings and a flashing gold-lettered sign is one of the old-timers in Bourbon Street. It was a part of the estate of Jean Baptiste Poeyfarré in 1824 but when it was erected has not yet been established. The balcony railing is a most attractive piece of cast iron.

542 BOURBON STREET—The low and quite evident ancient structure at the southeast corner of Bourbon and Toulouse was the property of Jean Baptiste Poeyfarré as long ago as 1808 but was probably erected long before that year.

OLD OPERA HOUSE SITE   BOURBON AND TOULOUSE

Little remains on this site to tell the visitor of the glory that once was that of the old French Opera House. A modern hotel now occupies this famous corner. Built in 1859 from designs by James Gallier, Jr., and Richard Easterbrook, this temple of song had a long career and a varied one until a fire in 1919 reduced the home of opera and Carnival balls to a mass of smoking embers and twisted iron. It was here that the immortal Patti electrified audiences and saved the initial season from failure.

Turn left into Toulouse Street for a moment to view an old structure that adjoins the opera house site.

828 TOULOUSE STREET—Bulking against the site of the old French Opera House is a mansion which is the admiration of visiting architects. Even such an eminent authority as the famed architect H. H. Richardson declared it to be the finest designed structure in New Orleans. The site was purchased January 7, 1836,

from Madeline Wiltz, by Mme Marianne Bienvenu, widow of Nicolas Godefroy Olivier, a wealthy planter of Saint Bernard Parish, and construction began immediately.

LANGEVINE'S SHOP   600 BOURBON ST.

The one-story structure at the northeast corner of Toulouse and Bourbon, which we shall note as we return to Bourbon Street to take up again our stroll down this thoroughfare, dates back into the Spanish period, as might be suspected after observing its construction. This reminder of the time when such a building was considered a pretentious shop in the Vieux Carré is an example of what was then called *une maison bâtie en colombage*, a construction of heavy timber framework, mortised and tenoned together, and covered with wide horizontal boards. This method of construction differed from the common *briquette entre poteaux* technique, which used brick as infilling between heavy timber posts.

Our records prove that René Théard, a builder, purchased the building on April 13, 1814, from Jean Louis Drouet. The latter stated that he had purchased the place in 1805 from Amedée Langevine, the probable original owner of the structure.

GAYARRE'S BOYHOOD HOME   601 BOURBON ST.

Our interest now is directed upon the northwest corner because here, in this same one-story plastered-brick building, a boy of eleven followed his mother into the recently purchased house where she was to eke out a living for herself and two young sons. The eleven-year-old youngster was a studious little fellow who became many years later the second of a trio of historians who chose Louisiana for the subject of their greatest work . . . these three immortals are Martin, Gayarré, and Fortier.

From September 26, 1816, to May 4, 1823, Charles Etienne Arthur Gayarré called this corner house home. His father had died three years before his mother (she who had been Marie Elizabeth Boré, the youngest daughter of the sugarmaker Etienne Boré) purchased this place. It was here she died a few months after her eldest boy reached his majority. Mrs. Gayarré's estate consisted of a score of slaves and this single piece of property. Charles Gayarré's boyhood home was an ancient structure when his mother became its owner, for some very ancient notarial documents inform us that Pierre Jourdan purchased it from Doña Luisa Cheval, the widow of Jean Millet, on May 13, 1777.

611 BOURBON STREET—Adjoining the old Gayarré home is a two-story brick residence which also counts its age well over the century mark. In 1808 it was the home of Jacques Lebrun.

619 BOURBON STREET—This residence has more than antiquity to make it an object of interest to those who know the history of the Battle of New Orleans, and to architects, for it was designed and erected by Arsène Lacarrière Latour, the engineer who designed the earthworks behind which Jackson and his army defeated

the British invaders in 1815. The owner of this site, who engaged Latour's services in 1812 for the erection of this home, was Pierre Roger.

624 BOURBON STREET—On the right-hand side of Bourbon Street is a house with its two balconies guarded by fine examples of wrought iron, and from the sidewalk a tunnel-like corridor leads to a spacious courtyard. It was built by Emile Péron, a refugee from Santo Domingo.

623 BOURBON STREET—One of the respected citizens of old New Orleans during the period of the Spanish domination was Don Esteban de Quinones, a public notary, in whose files were found many of the more important realty and business transactions that went on even long after the Americans swarmed into New Orleans. About 1795, Señor de Quinones selected this site for his home and built the combined residence and store that now occupies the site.

TRICOU RESIDENCE   711 BOURBON ST.

An old-time residence of the Quarter, one sure to catch the eye of the passerby, is the home which was the residence of the Wogan family. A heavy cypress gate bars the way to a characteristic courtyard which may be entered through the wicket in the *porte cochère*. It was erected by Joseph Adolph Tricou soon after he purchased the site, July 5, 1832, from Alexander Barron.

741 BOURBON STREET—The small one-story structure at the southwest corner of Bourbon and St. Ann streets, its old plastered-brick walls faced with weatherboards and covered with a double-sloping roof of slates with half-round Spanish tiles on the spines, is an old, old structure of the Vieux Carré, as one glance at the rear brick *cuisines* on the St. Ann Street side will mutely testify. The place was built January 27, 1787, by Don Luis Champigny. It was in this store that Francisco Juncadella and Pedro Font, the men who built the Old Absinthe House, carried on their first venture as commission merchants in 1802.

LAFFITE'S BLACKSMITH SHOP   941 BOURBON ST.

For more than a century this one-story brick-between-posts structure at the southwest corner of Bourbon and St. Philip streets has been pointed out as the famed smithy of the famous brothers Laffite . . . where Jean and Pierre Laffite carried on a feint of being *forgerons* although their business was not that of blacksmithing but the more genteel profession of smuggling cargoes of "Black Ivory" into the city. Pierre Laffite did the selling of slaves to the best folk in town, including the priests of the Cathedral and the Ursulines at their convent.

Much has been written about the Laffites, of their colorful piratical careers, of their patriotism when New Orleans was threatened by an invading British army, of their subsequent mysterious disappearance—so much so that fiction has completely distorted fact.

This so-called "Laffite Smithy," if you are interested in facts, was probably never put to such a use, in spite of the word on the iron plaque now decorating the Bourbon Street wall. It is, however, a very ancient structure—when it was built we do

not know. Our earliest record of transfer of ownership of the site dates back to 1772.

The place has had many owners but at no time did the name of Laffite or any of his men connected with his profession appear in any of the transactions having to do with this odd-appearing but typical structure of old, old New Orleans. What became of the Laffites?—of Jean, of Pierre, of their younger brother? No one really knows. All records, documentary records, on this phase of their careers are singularly lacking. One notarial act throws some light on this puzzle. It mentions Pierre's wife Françoise Sel—*"veuve de feu Pierre Laffite,"* she named herself—on November 26, 1834, when she asked permission to sell certain property to a planter from Vermillionville, as Lafayette, Louisiana, was then named.

New Orleans' notarial records, however, are literally filled with thousands of sales of slaves by brother Pierre. Jean's signature appears only occasionally, but in each case the surname is spelled "Laffite" (and not "Lafitte," which is the orthodox spelling) by the signatory. The claim that the Laffites were of mixed blood is demolished by the fact that in each case the notary, and they were careful about this in those days, did not identify any of the Laffites, nor Pierre's wife, as a person of color. A great deal of foolishness has been written about these smugglers—but probably a lot more will be foisted upon a receptive public.

Dominique You, so frequently coupled with the Laffite brothers, was in fact named Frédéric Youx. As he was a native of Santo Domingo, his followers called him "Captain Dominique"—just as some men are called "Texas Bill" or "Arizona Charley." He was a sailor and the fabulous tale that he was one of Napoleon's artillerymen has no foundation in fact.

1003 BOURBON STREET—The corner mansion, facing Bourbon Street and directly opposite the alleged "Laffite Smithy," is of comparatively recent construction; that is, when we compare it to many other structures in the Vieux Carré, for it was erected by P. J. Gleisses in 1849.

As there are not any residences of historical importance that lure us further along Bourbon Street, let us turn into St. Philip and make our return jaunt up Dauphine Street.

The grape design, a popular cast-iron balcony railing in the Vieux Carré

Up Dauphine Street

WE NOW TURN INTO Dauphine Street to continue up it in the direction of the main part of town. Here we will inspect the buildings that line this old thoroughfare which was originally named, according to some records, *rue Dauphiné* after the province in France, and not for the Dauphiness of the royal house.

LE PRETRE MANSION   716 DAUPHINE ST.

One of the landmarks of the Vieux Carré is the tall building at the southeast corner of Dauphine and Orleans streets noted both for the beauty of the cast iron that embroiders its many balconies and for the view of the rear of Saint Louis Cathedral seen through the lacework frame of the third-story gallery railing. We call it the Le Prêtre mansion, although Jean Baptiste Le Prêtre, a prominent merchant of New Orleans of a century and a half ago, did not erect the edifice. It was built in the fall of 1835 by Dr. Joseph Coulon Gardette, a dentist who came here from Philadelphia during Spanish rule and created a lucrative practice in old New Orleans. Four years after its completion he sold it for $20,049 to the merchant whose name it now bears.

Dr. Gardette married Zuliné Carrière, whose name was linked with that of Daniel Clark and it was their daughter who became the famous Myra Clark Gaines.

Gardette's new mansion became one of the showplaces of the old town, notable for its high basement, the first kind to be built here, and the cast-iron lacework that enclosed the balconies was admired then as today. In the spring of 1839 Le Prêtre became its owner and here he and his family lived for nearly half a century, until it was taken over by the Citizen's Bank in 1870.

PERE ANTOINE'S DATE PALM   837 ORLEANS ST.

Directly opposite the Le Prêtre mansion, in Orleans Street, where a wooden cottage occupies the site, was the once-noted spot where that beloved Capuchin priest, Fray Antonio de Sedella, had his lowly hut under a high date palm. This

147

Père Antoine's date palm as it appeared in 1841

palm tree, made famous in tales, especially in Thomas Bailey Aldrich's story, disappeared not so many years ago.

The famed Capuchin did own this spot, for a notarial act of February 20, 1811, tells us: *"Le Rev. Père Antoine Sedella, curé de la paroisse de Saint Louis de la ville et paroisse de la Nouvelle Orléans,"* paid Joachim Lozano 2,230 *piastres* for the site. He retained ownership until December 21, 1821, when he sold the place to Philippe Avegno. The only authentic picture of this famous date palm is the one drawn by Sir Charles Lyell in 1841 and reproduced in his works.

905 ORLEANS STREET—Before we leave this interesting corner, let us glance into Orleans Street at the building on the downtown side one removed from Dauphine. It was built in 1825 by Dame Marie Félicité Adélaide Jolly, the widow of François Hullin.

J. B. DEBOIS'S MANSION   631-633 DAUPHINE ST.

Few old houses in the Vieux Carré can boast a more unique or a more beautiful balcony railing of wrought iron than that decorating the gallery of the ancient structure at 631-633 Dauphine Street. As one glance tells you it is of considerable antiquity and some records appear to prove it was built in 1794 by Geronimo La Chapelle.

In 1816 Jean Baptiste Debois, a native of Chalon-sur-Saône, France, and for many years a prominent New Orleans attorney, purchased the home. In renovating the mansion the new owner placed on the balcony the fine wrought-iron railing that now decorates it. A feature is his elaborate *J B D* monogram in the center. Just above the graceful composition of initials will be observed the square and compasses of Masonry. Masons will note that the square and the compasses are the French symbol—the *G* being absent. The ancient mansion has fallen into "a long sabbath of sad decay" but Debois's bold monogram, his square and compasses, and

the little coiled snakes on either side of the central panel still defy the inroads of neglect and the corrosion of time and the elements.

MAJOR LATOUR'S SCHOOL   625-627 DAUPHINE ST.

The ancient *casa,* its in-curving roof covered with green tiles, is even older than the building next door for it dates back to a period that antedates the first great New Orleans fire. In the musty, termite-eaten records of that venerable *escribano publico,* Don Carlos Ximenes, we find that it was standing in 1789 when Gilbert Leonard became its owner, purchasing it from Don Juan Bautista Delmas. In 1811 he sold this house and its large courtyard to a pair of French engineers and architects who came to New Orleans a few years before to practice their profession.

Arsène Lacarrière Latour will always be remembered as the principal engineer to Andrew Jackson at the Battle of New Orleans, for it was Major Latour who selected the site for the mud earthworks behind which the American forces successfully contested the British shock troops on January 8, 1815. It was this same A. Lacarrière Latour whose *The War In West Florida and Louisiana* is the recognized basic authority for any account of that historic encounter. He was the architect who designed and constructed Dr. LeMonnier's mansion at Royal and St. Peter streets; he planned and built the first Orleans Street Theatre, and the Roger residence at 619 Bourbon Street, as well as a number of other old homes in the Vieux Carré. He was a graduate of the Paris Academy of Fine Arts and was as talented in his building operations as he was being an emergency army engineer.

Jean Hyacinthe Laclotte, his partner in the architectural work, was also a pupil of the same French academy. When the city was threatened with invasion, Laclotte volunteered as a private in the ranks and served from December 6, 1814, to January 4, 1815, when he was attached to the staff of General Jacques Villeré, who commanded the First Louisiana Militia. Laclotte's fame rests, too, with the Battle of New Orleans for it was he who made the original painting for the famous engraving that is reproduced so frequently in accounts of that historic feat of arms.

XIQUES MANSION   521-523 DAUPHINE ST.

At 521-523 Dauphine Street is a gray-painted brick building with high columns and double curving stairways leading from the sidewalk to the raised gallery of the first floor. In the 1930s and 1940s this mansion, planned by a master architect and built for a prominent Spanish-Creole family, was occupied by Vieux Carré nightclubs. It has seen many owners since the time it was built in 1851, and has been put to various uses—from private residence to gambling hall, from seltzer water plant to honky tonk—and its age and origin have been variously surmised.

In 1851 a wealthy Spaniard named Angel Xiques purchased the vacant lots and had J. N. B. de Pouilly design a residence which would reflect his importance in the community.

505 DAUPHINE STREET—This was John James Audubon's celebrated "little house in Dauphine street," where he and his family faced near starvation in 1821-22 when the bird artist was working on his now-famed *Birds of America*.

401 DAUPHINE STREET—The low, plastered-brick building, formerly but erroneously pointed out as "Audubon's Studio," was erected by Jean Puich soon after it was willed to him July 26, 1823, by a relative named Domingo Pi.

900 ST. LOUIS STREET—That the building now occupying the southwest corner of Dauphine and St. Louis streets is an old-timer is evidenced by its general appearance and construction. But further evidence is at hand to show that it was standing in 1807, for in April of that year Don Balderio Thomas Villaseca donated it to his daughter Eleonore when she married François Bru.

The French Market

EVERY VISITOR SHOULD INCLUDE the old French Market in his pilgrimage, for there is no more interesting or characteristic spot in New Orleans. The market-place had several buildings devoted to the business of supplying the folk of the Vieux Carré with foodstuffs, such as the Meat Market, Fish Market, Fruits and Vegetable Market, and the Bazar, each under its own roof and grouped in one place near the Mississippi River, a spot, so tradition informs us, first used by the Indians as a bartering place. Later the French here established their *Halle des Boucheries*. The first marketing structure was erected by the Spanish in 1791, but it was replaced in 1813 by a meat market. The other structures were built at a much later date, and the whole market was reconditioned by the city government in 1938-39, and again in 1974-75.

To reach the French Market the visitor can make a special pilgrimage or, when inspecting the Cathedral, Cabildo, and Pontalba buildings, walk through Jackson Square in the direction of the river and down Decatur Street, which was known as *rue de la Levée*. On our way we can note a few other historic buildings and sites.

MADAME BEGUE'S   823 DECATUR ST.

Opposite the historic French Market, and only a block away from the Square where General Andrew Jackson sits in perpetual politeness on his rearing bronze battle charger, is a modest brick building occupying the downtown corner of Decatur and Madison streets. It was here, not so many years ago, in a room on its second floor, that visitors to New Orleans enjoyed a distinctive "breakfast"—a Gargantuan feast that began at eleven in the morning and never ended before three in the afternoon!

This restaurant was known far and wide as "Madame Bégué's." It was here that she became famous—it was here that the food she cooked for discriminating palates became famous—it was here that Madame Bégué served meals that could be procured nowhere else, even in old New Orleans!

Famed as she was for her delectable French dishes, her *cuisine Créole*, Madame Bégué was a German. She was born Elizabeth Kettenring in Bavaria in 1831. In

151

The old French Market (drawn by Clarence Millet)

1853, a strapping *fraulein* of twenty-two, she landed in New Orleans to join her brother Philip Kettenring, a meat carver in the French Market. The young woman got a job in the kitchen of a small café opposite the market, Louis Dutrey's Coffee House, where the husky butchers from the market always went for their "second breakfast" at eleven in the morning. Here the German girl became adept in wielding a long-handled skillet over a hot stove.

It wasn't long before the young woman from Bavaria took a deeper interest in Dutrey's Coffee House for she became the wife of Monsieur Dutrey. She ruled the kitchen, her sceptor the long-handled skillet, while husband Louis mixed potables for the guests of the popular coffeehouse. It was her breakfasts, more than his toddies and cocktails, that brought fame to the modest brick building. When Louis Dutrey died in 1875 his widow kept the place going by her cookery. In 1877 Hypolite Bégué, a native of France who had been carving steaks in the market for the past nine years, was induced by the widow to tend bar for her. Three years later the name of the coffeehouse was changed from Dutrey's to Bégué's for, as may easily be guessed, Hypolite married the widow who was eight years his senior.

In 1885, at the time when New Orleans held its Cotton Centennial Exposition, Madame Bégué's was "discovered" by tourists and her breakfasts became known even outside the Crescent City. On October 16, 1906, the coffeehouse was closed for the first time in thirty-one years for Madame Bégué had laid down her pots and pans never to take them up again. Hypolite Bégué carried on alone for a short time only, for he married Françoise Lafforgue, widow of Jean Pierre Laporte, who had been the first Madame Bégué's assistant in the kitchen, and the place continued as "Madame Bégué's." In 1917 Hypolite joined Elizabeth Kettenring in the plot in Metairie Cemetery and the second Madame Bégué carried on the traditional breakfasts until the postwar depression struck. Then the famed breakfasts became memories.

Morning glory cast-iron balcony railing at 536 Dumaine St.

The sturdy brick building which housed the original Madame Bégué's was built in 1826 on the site of the old French, Spanish, and United States arsenal. It still stands at the selfsame corner, although the name *Bégué* is missing. Today it is called Tujague's, and here John Castet, who worked many years for Hypolite Bégué, preserved the place as one of the dining shrines of old New Orleans. (Bégué is pronounced "bay-gay" and Tujague's may be called "two jacks.") The original Madame Bégué's celebrated recipes were published in 1900 in a volume entitled *Old New Orleans Cookery.*

This whole square, from the rear of the Pontalba building line to Dumaine and Chartres streets, was the site of old French and Spanish arsenals and the notorious Condé Street quadroon ballroom. In 1826 it was divided into building lots and sold by the United States government. It was then that the narrow street named for President James Madison was cut through from Levee to Condé, as Chartres Street was then called.

LE VEAU-QUI-TETE 919 DECATUR ST.

Opposite the French Market is a two-story structure that occupies the site of two very old and popular coffeehouses of the past . . . Le Veau-qui-Tête, R. Revel's "The Suckling Calf" tavern, and, at a later date, it was the *Café des Réfugiés,* once the recognized headquarters of the *Colons de Saint-Domingue* when the refugees from Santo Domingo swarmed into New Orleans after the uprising of the blacks on that West Indian island. Here could be found West Indian strangers, *révolution-naires,* filibusters, maybe even pirates, a motley lot very fond of a distinctive and potent beverage called *le petit goyave.* This "little *goyave,*" brewed from the fruit of the guava shrub, had the power to make those who overindulged to wake up the morning after with a big—a very big—head. Revel's Suckling Calf tavern was doing business here from 1821 to 1825 at what was then 58 *rue de la Levée.*

HOTEL DE LA MARINE—Immediately adjoining the *Café des Réfugiés* and *Le Veau-qui-Tête* was the *Hôtel de la Marine,* or Navy Hotel, owned in 1809 by Jean Noël d'Estrehan and leased to Bernard Tremoulet who later became best known for his "Tremoulet House" at St. Peter and *rue de la Levée.* In 1815, F. Turpin was the manager of the *Hôtel de la Marine,* which was long a rendezvous of adventurous spirits and it was in this building that dozens of Sicilians were butchered in 1857 during the "Know-Nothing Riots," when race feeling ran high.

CAFE DES REFUGIES   514 St. Philip St.

Let us step aside for a moment into St. Philip Street to gaze upon this two-storied brick building which housed, many years ago, the celebrated *Café des Réfugiés.* This was the first location of this café which became a gathering place for all the strange folk which usually inhabit any cosmopolitan city's waterfront. Here it was, in 1808, soon after the house had been erected by Pierre Hurtubise, that Jean Baptiste Thiot opened his popular thirst-quenching emporium and christened it *Café des Réfugiés.* Here it was, too, that Thiot made popular a distinctive and potent beverage which he named *le petit goyave,* brewed from the fermented juice of the guava plant, toting the kick of an army mule and resembling the same sort of liquor known in Mexico as *pulque.*

Le petit goyave became an instant favorite and the usual tipple of the Laffite brothers, Jean and Pierre; "Captain Dominique" You, as Frédéric Youx was called; René Béluche, the smuggler; refugees from Santo Domingo; West Indian blacks; Kentucky flatboatmen; and all the other favorite figures of legendary and fabulous writers . . . if you want that sort of imagination mixed with facts. In 1833, when Pierre Hurtubise, Jr., sold the place with its peculiar *patio* to Jean Louis Arnaud for $16,100, host Thiot moved his *Café des Réfugiés* to the location already pointed out in *rue de la Levée* opposite the French Market. A year later he renamed it the "Pig and Whistle"—believe that or not!

CARRICK'S COURT—An interesting old building at 1023-1027 Decatur Street, which has a domed corridor leading to a rear court shared by the owners of four buildings, was erected May 28, 1828, by the widow of James Carrick and given this well-to-do merchant's name.

U.S. MINT   400 Esplanade

At the corner of Decatur Street and the Esplanade is the former United States

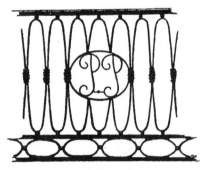

Balcony at 927 Toulouse St.

Courtyard of 628 Toulouse St. (drawn by Clarence Millet)

Mint, erected at a cost of $182,000 soon after Mayor Denis Prieur, on June 19, 1835, sold the government what was then "Jackson Square." This first park to be named for Andrew Jackson occupied the site of Fort San Carlos, where Old Hickory reviewed his troops on the eve of the several battles that saved New Orleans in 1815. The mint, which once turned out coin at the rate of $5 million a month, served as a federal jail given over during the days of World War II to the Coast Guard. It was in front of the mint that William Mumford was hanged in 1862 for tearing down the United States flag after the surrender of the city to Admiral Farragut's fleet. Mumford, sometimes described as a youth, was a grown man, forty-one years old. The building is now a part of the Louisiana State Museum complex and houses archival collections and historical exhibitions.

U.S. CUSTOM HOUSE   CANAL ST.

In Canal Street, near the Mississippi River waterfront, and occupying a whole city square, is the imposing government structure that in its century-old life has witnessed much of New Orleans history. The cornerstone of this granite-faced building was laid February 22, 1849, by collector of customs Denis Prieur, a former mayor of the city. It was not completed until some years later and cost $4 million. The huge building was not occupied by government offices until August 5, 1856, when the Custom Service under collector Thomas C. Porter moved in. It is the important government building in the Vieux Carré—although younger than the old mint. The superintendent of construction was Lieutenant P. G. T. Beauregard, U.S.A., who a few years later won undying fame in the Civil War as the most brilliant general who served the Confederacy. It was Beauregard who gave the order to open fire on Fort Sumter and thus began the four-year struggle between the North and the South. Visitors to New Orleans should visit the Custom House and inspect the famed Marble Hall on the second floor and study its many decorations.

Index